Now YOUR Turn For Success!

Training And Motivational Techniques For Direct Sales And Multi-Level Marketing

by

Richard Houghton and Janet Kelly

Crown House Publishing Limited

Published in the UK by

Crown House Publishing Limited
Crown Buildings
Bancyfelin
Carmarthen
Wales

First published 1997
by Syarikat Chip Seng Trading Sdn. Bhd.

British Library of Cataloguing-in-Publication Data
A catalogue entry for this book is available
from the British Library.

ISBN 1899836217

Printed and bound in Wales by
WBC Book Manufacturers,
Waterton Industrial Estate,
Bridgend, Mid Glamorgan.

Table Of Contents

List Of Figures

Acknowledgements

We would like to take this opportunity to personally thank everyone who assisted with the compilation of this book, and whilst there are too many to list here, we have singled out the following people for our particular thanks:

**Dato' Mustapa Mohamed, Gary Skillman,
Fred Marfleet, Amanda Lawrence,
Billi Lim, Jenny Houghton, Paul Southworth,
Jason Kelly and David Bowman.**

Foreword

Now It's YOUR Turn For Success! by Richard Houghton and Janet Kelly is a new book designed to help would-be entrepreneurs truly understand the exciting growth opportunities the Direct Selling industry can bring them.

There could not have been a more appropriate time for the release of this book, as many Direct Sales Companies are enjoying wonderful growth and sales success through their diverse range of quality products and dynamic sales and marketing teams.

Growth and success, however, don't just happen; they are created from experience, knowledge, training, commitment and energy linked with the fundamental desire for personal development and earnings potential.

Within this book all the above components of success are covered, and the reader will be able to follow a step-by-step process in search of their ambitions.

Enjoy your journey through its pages and take YOUR turn for success.

Paul Southworth
Chairman and Chief Executive
Tamarind International Limited

Preface

by Richard Houghton and Janet Kelly

Although born in England and Canada respectively, we were working and living in Malaysia when we discovered the need for an industry-based training guide on Multi-Level Marketing (MLM) and Direct Sales, including basic yet fundamental skills for new starters right up to network building, leadership, duplication and developmental skills for the experienced distributor. Motivational books and courses were available but rarely specific to the industry.

This prompted us to compile a comprehensive and motivational book on the subject, utilising our vast experience and many contacts within the industry. As MLM and Direct Sales is an International Industry the content of the book can generally apply in countries worldwide from South-East Asia, North America, Europe and almost any place in-between.

This book has been written for the benefit of anyone either interested in joining or who is already a member of a Multi-Level Marketing company or a Direct Sales company.

As we have been extensively involved in both types of company for a period totalling in excess of *thirty years* you can now benefit from our experiences by learning first-hand how to market and sell your company's products to the best effect, how to develop and increase your client base and your network (and your income), how to understand the basic concepts of what is known as a 'marketing plan' and what this could mean for you.

This book is *not* a biography or an 'easy way to make money'!

Although we have both independently held top achievers positions for our respective companies, one of which was the Top World-Wide Distributor, we have also learned of the many mistakes which people and companies have made and we will identify these for you to reduce the chance of you suffering the same fate. We now have our own UK-based training and consultancy company called **'Torgate Training & Consultancy Ltd.'** with contact offices in Canada and Malaysia and which provide specialist training within these industries.

This book is a simple yet fundamentally essential handbook on how each type of company generally operates, how you can establish and develop your 'own' successful business and how to apply the best methods to ensure you succeed in these industries. It could almost be viewed as a personal 'training guide' designed to help you achieve success. Some companies will take the content of this book and create their own training courses, such is the depth and breadth of its content.

If you were to read this book from cover to cover you would find there is some duplication within certain chapters; this is intentional, as the book has been written with the expectation that some readers will more readily want to focus their attention on specific chapters and as such may miss the benefits derived from many good examples, experiences and ideas which are provided throughout the book.

Where the term 'salesperson' is used this can also be taken to read: agent or distributor. And no specific inference is meant when stating 'he', for this should be read to equally relate to 'she', etc.

If you are currently associated with a Multi-Level Marketing company or a Direct Sales company, the content of this book will assist your understanding of not only what is required to succeed (you probably know that already) but more importantly *how* to turn your present performance into even greater success and personal enrichment!

Please read on, but make sure you have some spare paper to hand in order to take notes, for we feel certain that by following and implementing the sections contained within this book, and by adapting and interpreting them for your own company and its products or services, you will dramatically increase your opportunities for success because now it really is:

YOUR Turn For Success!

Chapter One

In The Beginning...

If you are reading this book because you are thinking of joining a Multi-Level Marketing (MLM) company or a Direct Sales company, welcome to what is likely to be an extremely informative, helpful and therefore beneficial book.

However, if you are currently already connected to one or more of this type of company then you will no doubt be inclined to move on to another chapter. Before you do so please take our advice and read the whole book, as for a small investment of your time you will undoubtedly discover new ideas and avenues within each section which could be of benefit to you when developing your network and which you may have previously not considered or even overlooked.

Firstly, we need to consider the newcomer to the industry, for there will be many considerations to take into account before you ultimately make the final decision – to join or not to join. One of the first considerations is the simple question – *why?*

Do you believe that by joining an MLM or Direct Sales company this will be the answer to all your prayers and that great riches will come your way with very little effort – *wrong!*

Or maybe you are one of those people who think that by taking advantage of the opportunity which has presented itself to you – joining – you can realise all your dreams and earn stacks of money to pay off debts, credit cards, overdrafts, etc. – *wrong again!*

Alternatively you could be the type of person who possibly does not have much in the way of debts but wants to dramatically increase your earnings, again with little effort – *wrong!*

Finally, you might be considering joining as a way to earn some money part-time whilst you maintain your normal job – *correct!*

We have found that quite often the best way to start in the business is to begin on a part-time basis and thereby maintain your regular income, as you develop your bank of customers and your business. This in itself will create greater demands on your time and also show increases in the level of income derived from it eventually leading to you taking a more full-time role. If you are joining on a full-time basis right from the start – don't worry, this can be and is a successful way to begin your new career. However, there are likely to be different requirements placed on you; and your discipline, focus and strategy in the new role will require more careful planning. More on this later.

If you intend joining solely to earn stacks of money with little effort you will be sadly disappointed. And if you already have debts and want to earn large sums of cash to repay them, again you will be sadly disappointed and more likely will see an increase in the extent of the debts you already have. That's not to say you will not earn money, for you can, but the amount you earn is likely to be directly related to the effort put in.

So what should you do?

We cannot answer this question for you on an individual basis but we will say that with any MLM or Direct Sales company they will expect (not unreasonably) for you to generate sales of their products or services. They may provide initial training and some support but this will vary from company to company and its effectiveness will also vary. Your immediate sponsor or recruiter will also provide some support but again this will vary in its effectiveness. Some are very very good and others will be so lacking in skills or the ability to transfer the skills, or even make the time for you, that you will be smarter to take control yourself.

It's quite advisable to take this action, as a result of the frequent inconsistencies which exist within the industry from company to company. To a large extent your earnings potential will be directly related to the level of training and support you receive on both the products and the skills to promote and sell them. Perhaps another question you should be asking yourself at this stage is "Exactly what level of support and training will be provided by the company?" If you have serious doubts about the level and extent of the necessary on-going training and support you are likely to receive, you might want to re-think about joining the company, for while there may be one company which does not provide adequate support for its members there will be many others who will.

One of the intentions of this book is to provide you with sufficient and adequate training or more precisely an understanding of what is required for you to be able to increase your chances of success should you wish to join an MLM or Direct Sales company.

Successful backgrounds

A question you may ask and which is often raised at recruitment meetings is:

"What is the best 'background' to have to ensure success?"

The term 'background' needs to take into account many different aspects and these will need to be considered more closely, i.e. occupation, financial, educational and personal.

Firstly, the good news here is that from various studies and across a wide range of companies there is not really one definitive previous occupation which will ensure success in either MLM or Direct Sales industries.

There have been many success stories from people who, before joining an MLM or Direct Sales company, were previously in one or more of the following occupations/industries, and with some hard work, concentrated effort and good training and support, developed their own successful businesses;

- ❖ Teacher
- ❖ Housewife
- ❖ Mechanic
- ❖ Doctor
- ❖ Real Estate
- ❖ Labourer
- ❖ Life Insurance
- ❖ Retail Staff
- ❖ Bank Manager
- ❖ Dentist
- ❖ Student
- ❖ Solicitor
- ❖ Milkman
- ❖ Farmer
- ❖ Accountant
- ❖ Hotel Staff
- ❖ Armed Forces
- ❖ Unemployed!

The list could go on for many pages and you will note from the examples shown above that there is a wide range of occupations and industries which previously held the attention of individuals; on a few occasions success has been derived by switching from one type of company – say Direct Sales – to say an MLM company; this is possibly due to the different ways each company is structured and the products they sell, but the point is they have now built on their skills and have been successful when joining the respective MLM or Direct Sales company.

This leads to another question – *why?*

We could spend a great deal of time discussing the whys and wherefores of how they became successful because there will undoubtedly be many factors involved. However, we suggest the reason for their success will, in reality, come down to just a couple of factors which will include; Attitude, Contacts and People Skills. However, the major one to consider here is:

ATTITUDE

In reality the reason people achieve success is because of their inherent 'desire to be successful' and their 'attitude' is very closely interlinked with this.

You will find later within this book sections relating more specifically to Attitude, Contacts and People Skills and how to utilise the people you know to best effect. But for the moment we would ask you to accept that if your mental approach and 'attitude' to the work or task to be completed is positive you are far more likely to achieve the desired results and much quicker than if you had a negative attitude.

Quite often you will observe a person, possibly within your own acquaintances or colleagues at work, who generally always seem to be cheerful, positive and fortunate (lucky). Invariably things work out well for them and you wonder how it is they always seem to get things to work out for them. To coin a well-used phrase – *You make your own luck.* The people who succeed do so because they 'make their own luck'. They strive to achieve a result and make the best of the result ultimately achieved, however close (or far) from the objective.

This relates directly to their attitude and an example of a useful phrase to remember is:

Things work out best for the people who make the best of the way things work out

Think about this phrase when you are next confronted with a situation which requires change to your life or habits or where you are required to complete a task the result of which you are not happy about. Learning to 'make it work for you' is very important to your mental attitude and achievements at work, at home and socially. But more on this later…

Another factor to take into account under the *'background'* heading is your present financial situation. This can be important because whilst attitude plays a major part in your potential for success, some of the attitude you may currently possess could be driven by your existing financial (and personal) situation.

Therefore, how *important* is it that you obtain sums of money by completing the sale of the products or services? (Bearing in mind the aim of selling these in the first place is to raise funds for yourself and/or your family).

If the answer to this question is *'very* important' or 'absolutely essential' then you will already be under a certain amount of pressure to sell. This pressure in itself is not necessarily a bad thing as it does provide a stimulus and motivation to act, but it does need to be controlled as it could have a detrimental effect on your success. We shall consider this and the implications in more detail later in the book. But for now, how effective will you be when confronted with a situation whereby the potential customer you are sat in front of is fully aware that you **need** to sell the product or service to meet this week's rent, credit card or hire-purchase payment?

Or, due to the financial pressures being placed upon you, very quickly your standards of honesty, integrity and ethics are forgotten and you make promises about the product or service which are untrue purely out of your absolute need to sell the product. This is *not* a recommended situation to find yourself in as you can be sure the days of making such claims and getting away with it will be seriously numbered. It does not take long for news of bad service and dishonest sales staff to spread amongst a community, and when you consider how much effort and time it takes to establish trust, honesty and integrity within a community in the first place it can be all too quickly destroyed in a moment of weakness; believe us, any short-term benefit derived is *not* worth the price. Therefore, as it is likely to be based around the perceived financial benefits associated with such work we suggest you think again why you are looking to join one of these companies.

Alternatively, it may be that your financial situation is reasonably sound and you are considering joining an MLM or Direct Sales organisation for other reasons (as outlined earlier); in this case you are likely to possess a slightly different attitude as you will be starting from a stronger financial standpoint.

You may have the desire to earn more money but do not have the absolute *need!*

For you the necessity to earn more income is not of paramount importance and may even be overshadowed by other events or needs in your life. If this describes your situation it's quite possible that you can identify with the former type of person but not necessarily directly relate to their situation, and *how hard can this job be anyway…?*

In view of this initial lack of need to earn the extra income you are likely to be less driven to achieve lots of sales. Not for you is the need to continually go out in search of new business and clients, you are just happy with the results you achieve. This is not meant to be and should not be taken as a criticism. There are many people who fit this scenario exactly and who have no specific need for large amounts of extra income and yet who regularly contribute consistent and, in some cases, significant amounts of production.

Large organisations, whether MLM companies or Direct Sales companies, depend to a greater or lesser extent on the consistent and regular production generated by this sort of agent or distributor.

They also depend on the consistent and regular production generated by those people who are not driven to increase the size of their network or team. They just do all they need to do every month. Again, there is nothing wrong with this sort of person although it is possible they have never been shown or understood the potential which exists for them to earn greater income and satisfaction within their organisation.

We shall consider these people later in the book. For now it is important just to recognise they exist and they form part of a much wider profile of different people with differing backgrounds that can all play a part in both their own success and the success of their chosen company.

Another factor to take into account when considering to join an MLM or Direct Sales company is the personal background of an individual. This relates to your personal and social lifestyle and is not associated with race, religion or any other barrier to forward-thinking people in a civilised world. What it reflects is your ability to 'get on' with other people. It does not matter if you are not the life and soul of the party, what matters is that you can readily talk to other people and thereby freely explain your company's products or services.

This is not a skill many people possess without training, so if you stop and think for a moment that you do not have these skills and therefore could not fulfil the role of a sales-person/distributor/agent, do not fear; by reading this book you will uncover many skills that you possess without realising it, and with constant practice will develop new competence and confidence which will increase your chances of success.

We have been asked if your zodiac star sign or the year in which you were born has any significance to the chances of you being successful, and once again we have to dispel such a rumour; there is no definitive evidence to support the theory that if your star sign was, say, Virgo, or, you were born under the year of the Snake, you stand a greater chance of succeeding. It simply does not make any difference which star sign you were born under, or in which year; what matters is your inherent *'Desire to be Successful'* and your *'Attitude'*.

Whilst still on the subject of people's background let us ask a question: "Do you believe that to succeed within an MLM or Direct Sales company you must be very intelligent, highly educated and possess a string of degrees and diplomas?" Alternatively, do you believe that people join such companies because they cannot obtain any other kind of employment and they have not been able to hold on to a job for longer than three weeks, therefore are likely to be at the other end of the intelligence spectrum?

Well, in truth both statements could be deemed as correct!!

Let us explain...

As you will have noted from the earlier pages, the wide range of occupations people previously held before they joined and became successful within either an MLM or Direct Sales company clearly shows that your *background* plays much less of a part in your success than some would have you believe. You will have noted that highly qualified people like Doctors, Solicitors and Dentists have become very successful. However, look closer at the list and you will notice that so too have Housewives, Labourers, Retail Staff and even the Unemployed!!

So amassing a wealth of academic qualifications in themselves is not a guarantee of success, but equally the lack of them is not a recipe for failure! It all comes down to the other key factors mentioned earlier – Attitude, Contacts and People Skills.

So, as you will have seen, the background of an individual is not as important as you may have previously believed. It makes little difference if you were a clerk in a bank or a top-flight executive, or maybe a taxi-driver, builder or a finance director. Individuals from any one of these occupations can succeed when provided with the right training, motivation, people skills, and who ultimately possess the *right attitude!*

The financial and personal background will have an effect also but largely only to the extent of the need for extra income and the motivation this invariably produces.

We would expect that within the pages of this book you will already have seen someone or something which relates to you and your background or to the background of someone you can relate to. Some people get hung up on their past and you often hear comments like: "I could not do that because I've only done xxxx before" or "How can I work for such a prestigious company as ABC when I've only ever done yyyy?" You need to cast these doubts aside and focus on what you want.

This is important because where your background is concerned in order to guarantee you the greatest opportunity to increase dramatically your chances of success, you must appreciate that it's not so much where you have been that is important but more, where are you going now and specifically *where do you want to be in the future* – create a 'vision' and work towards achieving it. You will be building something to aspire to, something to aim for, something which must be achievable and attainable and yet something which will motivate you each day to go out and take the next step towards achieving it. Only you can do this and reading this book will greatly assist in creating your own 'vision' and thereby ultimately increase your chances of success.

Products and services

When considering to join an MLM or Direct Sales company another question you should be asking yourself is "What are the products or services offered by the company, are they reasonably priced and do you like them?" The type and range of products or services offered by the company will also be an important and necessary factor for you to consider. If you do not like the product or can't relate to the services offered it will prove to be much harder to convince a potential customer of their worth.

How much easier it will be to promote something when you like it! Think of an item which you really like; a car, a perfume or a particular suit, for instance. When you talk about it to your friends we expect you will be confident, excited and enthusiastic.

How much easier it is to promote something you like, trust and believe in, so why not work for a company where you will be selling such products or services? Remember, companies which are product-driven and not solely opportunity-led, are generally more successful long-term.

If you enjoy using the products or services yourself this will be conveyed when you talk to others about them. Therefore you will be much more convincing. If you take a minute to think about the last time you bought something of value, was the salesperson confident about the item, excited and enthusiastic? We expect so because if not you most likely will have gone elsewhere to buy.

In order for you to maintain your own enthusiasm, confidence (and excitement!) for the products or services it will be very important for you to continually buy and use the relevant products your company supply as this shows both commitment and belief in the product. This is simple if the product in question is a consumable and repeatable item – washing powder or perfume – but requires more thought and conviction when it involves less consumable items or services or in fact items which are not directly repeatable – vacuum cleaners or water filters. In the example of the vacuum cleaner you will only be making such a purchase once in several years so make sure it's the right one! You can then speak volumes to a potential customer when, should they be undecided whether or not to buy, as you personally own the same or similar model and have experienced how effective it is, you will be far more convincing and persuasive.

Therefore, in most situations it will be possible to buy the company's products for personal use, and this is highly recommended to ensure you set a good example both to potential customers and to any potential new recruit you may be encouraging to join the organisation.

The price is an important factor also. If the products or services are very expensive how likely are you to be able to sell large quantities of them? If you bought them because of their superior quality, reliability or reputation, or possibly because you always believed in the 'you get what you pay for' philosophy, that is fine because others may also buy for the same reasons. Quality is quite often an important part of the buying decision after all. We all want the 'best that money can buy', or at least the best we can afford!

However, if you would not buy the products or services because of their poor finish, poor packaging, poor coverage, poor after-sales support or poor reliability how can you expect others to buy the products?

Chances are, they will not!

And when these thoughts go through your mind you should consider looking elsewhere for the company you want to represent.

This is not to say that everything you should consider selling has to be a high ticket item (expensive). Occasionally you will find that many of the lower priced items marketed by many companies represent extremely good value for money and when bought in bulk can show big savings.

This in itself can be quite an attractive proposition to some people and on the basis they like the product (or service) they will indeed buy in bulk and make the savings.

This is fine when you are dealing with the sort of products or services where quantity and price are all important; for instance, if you buy ten bottles of weight-loss tablets you can secure a bigger discount than if you bought only one bottle, or where you could buy four months' supply of washing powder instead of one month's.

Eventually these products will all be used but you still have to pay for them *now!* So consider what value the discount represents to you and if it shows significant savings and you would take up the offer it's quite likely that others will too. This means that you should buy all of the products or services which the company in question has to offer, that relate to you and your family's needs. This shows your commitment to and belief in your selected company. We shall discuss some of the other benefits of this process in more detail later.

By applying the rule of 'If I like it, believe in it and would buy it, why shouldn't others?' you can get an indication of the likelihood that the company in question has a range of products which you could quite possibly sell to a multitude of different people, starting with the people you know.

This leads us to another question to ask: "How many people do I know that I could talk to and hopefully sell the products or services to?"

How many people?

It is important to realise that the most successful people within either industry are those people who know or come into contact with the most people. They do not necessarily sell the products to each and every person but more precisely encourage the people to join the network and thus sell the product for them! If you know only a few people locally, in your village or suburb say, then it will take a long time for the good news about the range of products you will have available to spread, thus increasing the number of people who could buy the products or services.

Although the potential for the greatest success rests with the people who know lots and lots of other people do not be too dismayed if you only know a handful of people, because of the small number (ten or twenty people?) that you do know, each will know different people from you and quite soon the number of people available for you to talk to will expand rapidly. Perhaps an example might help.

> If you spoke to just two people who in turn each spoke to two different people how many people would be aware of your products by the time the tenth set of people had been spoken to?

> An amazing **1024.**

> And even more amazing is that if you carried this on for another ten times the number increases to **1,048,576.**

This calculation is called exponential, but don't worry about the name; just think about how by talking to just two people and for each of them to talk to a further two people the number of potential people aware of what you have to sell increases dramatically.

Significantly over one million people could be aware of what you hope to sell or promote in a relatively short space of time providing they all tell just two people each over a series of twenty. This is not selling the product or service yet, just discovering the potential number of people you could be talking to about it.

But there is even more good news. Based on a study carried out in Europe a few years ago you might be surprised to learn how many people you actually do know of. Although we stated earlier that you may only be starting from a position where you knew a limited number of people (ten to twenty) in your local area, in reality you do know a great deal more people than this, a far *greater* and significant number of people than this.

Let us explain – try this simple exercise…

Take a piece of paper and write down the names of everyone you know. Easier said than done? Well, to start with let's focus on your immediate family, your spouse's (or partner's) family, your children's contacts, your friends, relations and work colleagues, either in this country or anywhere else in the world. This may take some time for you to complete but it will be worth it (time well spent!).

Now how many does this add up to?

Next, start to write down the names of people in your social life, members at your social clubs, societies, Round Table, Rotary, fitness club, golf club, car club, bridge club, etc., even where you worship. Add these names together and you will be surprised how many you have accumulated already and we are not even halfway to arriving at the total number of people you know yet!!

So far all of the people you have listed are people where you know their name. Now start to list all of the people where you don't know their name but where you see or meet them regularly and they are 'known' to you. Quite possibly you nod your acknowledgement to them from across the street or over a counter in a shop or they may be neighbours whom you see every day and wave to but you don't know their names (yet!).

There will be many of these sort of people, for instance: people you regularly meet at the stores where you shop, where you fill the car up with petrol, where you have your hair done, where you have the car serviced, where you buy your newspaper, where you pay your bills each month, where you bank, where you deposit your savings, where you have stationery printed, etc., etc.

The list is virtually endless… but how many does your list finally add up to?

You may be surprised to learn that the survey we mentioned earlier revealed that when taking into account *all* of the above different types of people the average thirty-five-year-old actually 'knows' it reaches over *twenty-five thousand people* (25,000). This is likely to be even higher the older you are. We think you will agree that is a lot of people.

Don't be disappointed if your particular list falls short of this number because the survey took into account every possible eventuality; even people you speak to when booking a flight or a holiday or when arranging for an eye test or simply considering the people you come into contact with who refer you to others. Essentially, we are not talking about the vast number of people who you do not know in any shape or form, but more precisely what the survey concludes is that the above people are all people you know to a greater or lesser extent and therefore qualify for inclusion under the rules of the survey.

The exciting news that comes out of all this and what this could really mean to you is that the earlier number quoted for some readers of ten or twenty people are likely to be people you would consider you know, and know well. What the survey tells us is that in reality we know (and know of) a far greater number of people than we perhaps at first realise.

Now just think how the exponential calculation we did earlier could work for you when relating it to the list you have compiled in front of you; every one of these people will know other people and each one only needs to refer just two people to you…

"How hard can it be?" "How hard do you want it to be?"

The above sections of the book are very important to cover *first* because you need to be clear as to why you are considering joining an MLM or Direct Sales company and if you have the necessary aptitude and ability to succeed – although how you define 'success' is something you need to be clear about. Many people join in the belief "How hard can it be?" and we could answer this by stating "How hard do you want it to be?"

Firstly, let us consider the various ways different people state what represents success;

☺ no financial worries – financial security
☺ recognition from your peers – accolades & awards
☺ regular holidays abroad – two or three a year
☺ a good quality car – Mercedes, BMW or Jaguar
☺ a large house – maybe detached with four to five bedrooms
☺ ownership of other material things – boat, house overseas, an island!
☺ private education for your children – at the best schools/university
☺ private medical care – for you, your family and your grandparents
☺ a successful business of your own!

There may be other areas which you believe represent success for you and that's fine, write them down now whilst you think of them. Possibly you only think one or two of the above areas represent success for you and that's fine too. It does not matter what we think represents success; it is what *you* think represents success that is important as this is one aspect which will motivate you to achieve it.

All of the above can and have been achieved for the top performers within MLM or Direct Sales companies and we do not intend to include within this book pages of other people's stories of their successes, we shall leave it up to them to write their own book. What you need to appreciate is the time, effort, persistence and money which these individuals contributed and invested in their particular business to achieve the success attained.

Many people who are considering joining or who have in fact already joined and have been within their particular company for some time often look at these successful individuals and say: "If they can do it so can I" and "How hard can it be?" Well, it can be hard, it can be tough and it can be lonely. But if you act on the information contained within the chapters of this book it will be none of these things and you will without question dramatically increase your chances of success.

As stated above: "How hard do you want it to be?" Too many people make life difficult for themselves by not following simple yet rudimentary rules of operation; they become dispirited, disillusioned and leave dissatisfied. What a shame and what an unnecessary loss!

No doubt some of the blame for this loss is likely to rest with their recruiter, sponsor or manager. It may be the individual joined for the wrong reasons as outlined to you earlier, or, and what is most likely, they just did not follow the simple *'steps to success'*. We are certain they will have striven for success but, unbeknown to themselves, made life very difficult due to their lack of knowledge about the steps to success which we shall share with you shortly within this book.

But before we do let's next consider what these areas of success will bring you aside from the material things mentioned above. We have considered the various factors and questions you should ask yourself, all associated with joining an MLM or Direct Sales company. Now it might be helpful to consider the many other benefits to be gained from joining such companies, benefits which may not currently be available in the position you presently hold;

- ✓ a tremendous opportunity to achieve the things you want from life
- ✓ obtain extensive job satisfaction
- ✓ make many new friends
- ✓ establish an extensive circle of like-minded work colleagues
- ✓ develop long and lasting business relationships
- ✓ secure a better quality of life for you and your family
- ✓ potentially obtain improved health – some companies offer nutritional foods
- ✓ localised or world-wide travel for you and your spouse/partner

✓   greater spiritual and personal satisfaction
✓   increased stimulation and motivation
✓   witness some of the world's best speakers to assist with motivation and direction
✓   extend your personal, physical and mental development
✓   become part of one of today's most successful business enterprises

...and all of this from joining the right company for you and committing yourself to achieving nothing less than 100% success!

So you've reviewed all of the above and your decision has now been made, or has it? Before you rush out and sign anything let's just consider some of the differences between a Multi-Level Marketing company and a Direct Sales company.

Broadly speaking there are few main differences between the way in which they operate. They both need people to promote and sell their products or services and they are both in business to make a profit.

In effect an MLM company is a form of Direct Sales in that you will be selling a range of products or services. However, there are some specific differences and we have listed below some of the more common ones which relate to a reasonably new agent or distributor for you to check out; although this list is not meant to be definitive it will provide you with a reasonable guide. You will also find within other chapters of this book other similarities between the companies identified.

We would strongly advise you to check the specific details relating to any company you are considering joining, as they may vary from the list shown on the next page. Although our list is helpful it must only be viewed as a useful guide.

See below for explanations	MLM	Direct Sales
Payment made by a fixed salary, but low	No	Yes
Commission or payment on personal sales	Yes	Yes
Discount on personal purchases	Yes	Yes
Higher level discounts when targets met	Yes	No
Commission on recruiting new agents	No	No
Commission on % of new agents' sales	Yes	Yes
Training and support	Yes	Yes
International sponsoring	Possibly	Yes
Incentive packages – holidays/conventions	Yes	Yes

Fixed salary: At the time of printing we are not aware of any MLM company providing a straight salary as this conflicts with their method of operation. Direct Sales companies can offer a salary but when they do this is usually very low so as to encourage you to sell their products and thereby earn commission.

Commission payment on personal sales: The payment of commission by MLM companies is usually related to a variety of bonuses that are dependent upon the individual marketing plan of each company (see Chapter Two for more details). It is quite common for Direct Sales companies to offer commission payments.

Discounts on personal purchases: An MLM company will offer a discount on the purchase price of the goods to enable the distributors to secure some profit for themselves, or give them incentives to buy more products for personal use. A Direct Sales company may also offer some form of discount on the price of the products purchased by the agent although this is usually fixed and only available to the agent and/or their immediate family (if at all).

Higher level discounts when targets met: All MLM companies will generally offer an additional discount on the purchase price of the goods once certain targets have been achieved, thereby allowing the distributor to secure an even greater profit (see Chapter Two for more details on this process). A Direct Sales company will not generally offer any further discounts than those already mentioned.

Commission on recruiting new agents: The Pyramid Selling Act prohibits the direct payment of commission when recruiting (see Chapter Two for more information on this Act).

Commission on % of new agents' sales: This is quite normal in both industries although the extent to which you receive your percentage will vary and be dependent on certain targets having been met. One advantage MLM companies offer is the fact they will have many different levels from which the commission can be applied (see Chapter Two for more details on this method).

Training and support: Both industries will offer some form of Training & Support for their agents or distributors although the quality will vary quite extensively from one company to another. It is largely with this thought in mind, and having experienced some of the training available, we chose to write this book to assist you!

International sponsoring: On the basis the company is international then most MLM companies will allow you to sponsor internationally and this will provide a means of earning from distributors within your network who live in other countries around the world. You may be paid in either your own or the local currency and this will depend on the company. With Direct Sales companies it is possible to have an international arrangement but not all companies provide this facility.

Incentive packages: Both types of industry will offer an incentive package for its agents or distributors to encourage them to sell more and reach higher target levels, recruit more new members and maximise their own potential. Such incentives will normally take the form of prizes and free gifts or overseas holidays (which invariably include a convention or seminar). Each company will vary the location of its holiday/convention every year but you can be certain that it will be spectacular and well worth attending!

So as you can see from the above information, you really do need to do your homework and research each company in turn to satisfy yourself that both the company and you are likely to succeed.

Ask yourself a few more simple questions:

- what is the background of the company?
- do they provide any support or training? if so, how relevant is it and how often does it occur?
- will they assist with product training?
- if so, how effective is it and who will be taking the sessions?
- can I achieve the target set (if any)?
- how successful have other people become (ask for evidence)?
- what, if any, restrictions are there – only allowed to work locally, maximum earnings attainable, minimum products to be sold each month, etc?

Hopefully the above information will assist you when considering your choices and the options available. It is likely there will be other differences from one company to another in addition to those shown above and it is incumbent upon the reader to check out the specific details of their particular choice. This section is merely designed to provide you with an appreciation of a few of the differences; in reality there may be many more. New companies arrive in the MLM and Direct Sales industry on a regular basis, and they will each have something slightly different to offer, especially as they want (and need) to attract as many distributors as they can. Therefore, consider very carefully what it is that you want and satisfy yourself the company can deliver, always providing of course that you do!

The method of payment by an MLM or Direct Sales company to its agents/distributors is one of the most common differences. Therefore, the next chapter is devoted specifically to distinguishing these differences in more detail and thereby allow you to appreciate exactly how you are likely to be paid. After all, before you can spend your new income you first have to earn it and knowing how to earn the most from each company's system is important.

Learning Points From Chapter One:

1.   Why is your attitude more important than background?

2.   Is the company you are looking at product-driven?

3.   If you have joined an MLM or Direct Sales company, have you purchased products for yourself and family?

4.   It is important to compile a list of the people you know. If you haven't already started to create the list, now is a good time to do so.

5.   Know and understand the differences between an MLM company and a Direct Sales company.

Notes:

_____

_____

_____

_____

Chapter Two

Is That What I Can Earn?

Many people are confused about the various methods of payment structures which exist in the Direct Sales and MLM companies. Added to this, the names given to the payment structure will vary from Direct Sale to Direct Sale company, and also MLM to MLM company. Some of the common names used are: Commission Structure, Marketing Plan, Compensation Plan, Reward Package, Commission System and Payment Structure. The name isn't really important, it is what earning potential it provides for you and how well you understand and apply it that is important.

In the previous chapter we highlighted some of the differences between an MLM company and a Direct Sales company. What this chapter aims to show you is how the most common types of payment schemes operate and the subsequent benefits which can be derived by both you and the company. In subsequent chapters you will discover further differences between each type of company, but for now let's concentrate on the various payment methods adopted.

Direct Sales companies

Direct Sales companies generally tend to reward the agents in a very straightforward way – rate of commission for the products or services sold. If a target is met, then sometimes there will be a bonus. Sometimes there will be targets to meet over a period of time, and at the end of this period the bonus is paid.

We are aware of one company that runs an annual bonus scheme, and this works quite well for both the agent and the company. From the company's perspective, it helps to retain the agents, as they will be reluctant to leave a company if there are moneys still to be earned. From the agent's perspective, they know that at the end of the period they could receive a substantial cheque that could be used for holidays, car purchase, children's education, or possibly just invested!

Most of the plans for product-driven companies will be structured to give the distributor the best possible commission, based on a combination of retail sales and recruiting. Your reward comes in a balance of personal sales, and also the sales of the people you recruit. The products should be consumable, and repeatable. This will help in your recruiting of new distributors. The price of the products needs to be comparable to similar products found in shops. You need to ask yourself the question, 'Am I getting value for my money, and will my customers, who pay retail, also get value for money?' If you can answer yes, then give the marketing plan closer examination.

MLM companies

As with Direct Sales companies the method of paying distributors within an MLM company's structure will vary from one company to another.

Paying the downline

There are several MLM companies in existence that do not pay the distributor/agent directly, but rather pay the Key Leaders and expect them to pay the commission to each and every one of the downline that will have earned this commission based on the volume created during the period in question.

The company will remit a cheque to the Key Leader along with a print-out of the volume and/or sales figures of the members of the downline that will be entitled to payment. Then the person will remit a smaller cheque to each and every person in their organisation that is entitled to receive payment. Accompanying this cheque there should be some printed backup of how the cheque amount was calculated.

This situation, if handled correctly, poses no problems. However, you need to remember that your sponsor, or someone you have never met, will be responsible for paying you the moneys earned from your efforts.

If the company that you are considering joining operates under this method of payment, you need to ensure that there are no problems with payment from your upline, and also you need to verify that any copies of cheques of moneys earned by your prospective sponsor that are shown to you as 'achievable earnings' are cheques that relate to income earned by him as an individual, and not the cheque that reflects the total commissions earned by that particular network within the organisation.

'Get rich quick' schemes

"Opportunity can come disguised as hard work – you need to be prepared for it"

It must be stated that a plan that gives you unrealistic income for virtually no work should warrant much closer examination, unlike the phrase we have highlighted. These types of plans are generally created for the benefit of the company. Most times the company is new, and if you ask questions, sometimes you will find the people heading the company have been involved in another MLM company. Or, worse still, the directors of the company have no experience in MLM, and are not prepared to understand how the system works. All that these people know is that other companies are operating an MLM system, and they appear to be making a lot of money.

You may think that this is highly unlikely, but we can tell you from experience that this situation can happen not once, but two or three times in a short space of time! One such situation arose where the company director closed a company down on a Friday, and on the Monday morning, opened another company selling the same product!

People were gullible enough to join the second company, having lost money on the previous company! Needless to say, the company folded within a short space of time, and another venture was tried, but this time selling another product.

The way to help yourself eliminate this situation from happening to you is to ask the person who is recruiting you who the people are that head up the company. What do they know about them? You also need to know what MLM or Direct Sales experience do they have? Not surprisingly, there are a number of people out there who are of the belief that if you can obtain a product at a relatively inexpensive price, put a marketing plan together, sell the product at an inflated price, for a short period of time, they will make a fortune. They will undoubtedly make a profit, but the distributors are likely to lose the money that they invested in products and literature. Also too the customers who may have prepaid for their products. If they pay the distributor, and he in turn orders products in good faith, everyone will lose. Would you trust the distributor with an MLM product again in the future? Not many customers would.

Another situation that we have come across is the company owner who thought that if he supplied products at a low price, and paid bonus cheques at a somewhat consistent time of the month, that was his responsibility over. If you come across a company with this philosophy, it may well be in your best interest to pass it over.

Why should you pass this over? From experience, what you may find is that there is limited literature available. Literature, both highlighting the products and the business opportunity, are an important part of every MLM company. If the quality of the literature appears poor, it does not give a good impression to prospective distributors and potential customers. Also, it may be that the people heading up the company have little or no MLM experience, and therefore have no appreciation of the need for good quality literature, and prompt payment of all bonuses to the various people in the company who are generating a substantial amount of business, and ultimately putting money in the pockets of the owners.

It is important that the marketing plan be well balanced both for the distributor and the company, but also there must be more 'give' from the company. There should be a good training programme in place. The training should give the 'foundation' training, that is, the basics about the company, the products and the initial steps of the marketing plan. Second, you need to look at the ongoing training, what assistance is there for leadership training, duplication and motivation?

New vs established

When you are looking at the various companies that operate under the MLM system, you will undoubtedly come across a number of companies that have been around for a long period of time. These companies are established, and the networks are usually quite established too. Also, there are quite a number of individuals who are earning a very good living from their efforts.

You may ask yourself the question, "Do I want to be involved with a company everyone knows about?" You may think that because the company is established, then so too are the customers. You may think that the distributors within the organisation have quite a number of customers, and as customers are needed to help generate your personal volume, you may not be able to find new customers. This is wrong inasmuch as there are always new customers, existing distributors may move, or even the fact that some distributors do not use any form of follow-up when they have retailed the product, thus losing contact with their customers.

Another point to bear in mind when looking at an established company is the fact that as they are *established,* and the public know about them, their products are accepted, the price is accepted, and their method of sales is accepted. The history of the company will act as your advertisement for the promoting of the products.

If you are contemplating joining an established company and building an organisation, you may feel that because the company has been running for a number of years that everyone will have heard about the company and not want to join. Quite possibly they had been a distributor in the past and are no longer involved, or they had been approached with the opportunity and for whatever reason said 'no' to the opportunity at that time.

There is no need to worry about this situation because time does not stand still, and possibly the reason why the opportunity was turned down no longer applies, or their situation has changed to allow them to give the company a second look. What is important is that they are now in a position to accept the opportunity, or at least take a more serious look at it.

It is important to note that most companies have a rule that states a period of time must lapse before someone re-joins the company under a new sponsor.

If you look at some of the new companies that are being started, you may find that some of them have products that are similar to each other. You may wonder, if that is the case, surely there will be no ability for the new company to be successful? This is not the case, because each and every company is different. Their philosophies may differ, the remuneration plan may differ, they may be looking at international expansion, and most important of all, the products may be similar to another, but they are *not* the same.

If you are looking at a new company, you need to determine how competitive is the retail price of the product, because you need customers, and you also need to seriously look at the marketing plan to determine what the potential income could be. If you look at the possible income, you need to determine if the requirements to attain that income are realistic.

By joining a new company you may find recruiting very easy, but you need to look at the calibre of recruit – are they joining because they are positive about the earning potential within the MLM concept, and feel that they will enjoy some amount of success? Or are they merely joining because they repeatedly told you the reason they left their last two companies was because it was so hard to recruit and retail the products, or the company was wrong? You need to be careful if your recruit falls into the latter category, as these individuals are looking for the 'easy' way, and if they do not make an instant success for doing virtually nothing, they will leave and go on to the next company.

The products

If the company has a limited number of products, you need to know what else is on the horizon. Are there going to be new products introduced at some time in the future? You will need to know this, so that you can plan your strategy for customers and recruits. If there are going to be new products introduced, this is an ideal means to keep in touch with your customers, and the recruits who have not been producing sales.

It can be very reassuring to know that a company is going to launch new products. This clearly shows that the company has the foresight to look ahead, and makes the best use of the network of people who are distributing the products. Also, which products they are launching will be an indication as to the future planning of the company. You need to make sure that the future products are innovative and needed by the masses. What you don't want to see launched is an old product that has been replaced by modern technology, and the only reason it is the 'new' product is that the company was able to get a warehouse full of the products for virtually no money.

When a new product is introduced, this is the ideal time to contact all the customers who may have purchased your products, and for whatever reason, there is no longer a need. If they bought from you in the past, and they were happy with the quality and price, why shouldn't you contact them again about a new product?

The same can be said about your distributors in the network who may not have generated the sales that you and they had antici-pated. Maybe the product wasn't as easy for them to sell as they had first imagined. There is the possibility that a new product may be the means to help them get a boost. Also, if your network is producing a good amount of sales each month, the introduction of a new product will give your group sales a tremendous boost. Just think about how many people are in the network, and they buy products for personal use, and to sell to their customers.

We know of one top distributor with a worldwide organisation in over twenty countries that whenever the company introduces a new product, his monthly bonus cheque increases at a phenomenal rate. Everybody buys the product for personal use, and they also order the product to have a small supply of stock on hand for their customers. To get an understanding of this, think of how much your cheque would be if you had an organisation of over ten thousand members, and only half of them ordered £100 of the product. Take the commission amount from the company you are currently involved with, or the company that you are looking at joining. Are you impressed? This person we have mentioned has tens of thousands of distributors worldwide!

The company advantage

On the other hand, there are some plans that are only meant to have a short lifespan, and are merely a short-term cash fund for the person who 'created' the plan.

We mentioned earlier about the people at the head of some companies who spend most of their time creating plans that are just for their personal gain. They make the marketing plan and the product appear so simple, and the products so great. When reality steps in, the plan is complicated, the products are not good value for money, and the distributor loses heart and leaves.

Several things happen then. Firstly, the company don't have to pay out the total commission that they stated they would pay, because the person never reached the high levels to receive top commission.

Secondly, if the distributor leaves, he or she generally leaves the recruits with the company. Sometimes, they will still continue to order products, but this can be short-term because all too quickly they realise that the plan is not one that will give them the income they anticipated.

Another point that you need to examine is the total payout by the company. Many companies will shout about how much commission they pay out compared to another company selling a similar product. Take a closer look. Are they comparing like for like? Specifically, are they relating retail to retail, and wholesale to wholesale? Are the commissions payable before local taxes? Also, are the commissions based on the retail price, or are they based on a personal or group volume figure that is below the retail?

We recently came across a company that stated they paid a certain percentage of commission to distributors that was higher than several other companies selling comparable products. On closer examination, the commission payable was based on a personal volume that was less than the recommended retail price. The result was that the commission was lower when comparing retail for retail with the competitors. A very good marketing tactic that was in the company's favour!

The remuneration plan

The remuneration plan of any company must be such that it is fair to both the distributor and the company. Misleading the general public about the income potential will not help the company build a solid foundation from which to grow. There are a number of companies that have been in existence for more than thirty years, and have grown worldwide. These companies have built their foundation on consumable, repeatable products, that are fairly priced for the general public. The income potential has been clearly defined, and to date, tens of thousands of people have at one time earned a good income from the sales that they have generated.

The companies that have been running for over thirty years and are utilising the MLM system, have given thought to what they want to achieve – long-term credibility, by way of good products, a fair remuneration plan, and training. There has been an investment in both time and money to encourage the distributors to earn from the sales they create, and also the other people that they recruit to the company to also sell the products.

Remember, in order to earn an income from the sales of those people you recruit, you must have personally generated a pre-determined amount of sales yourself.

So how does the remuneration plan work for a Multi-Level Marketing company? There are several plans in existence that cover in one form or another what are known as: a Step Plan, a Binary System and a Matrix Plan. Each plan has both good and not so good points, and it is up to each individual to examine the plan of their chosen company in detail. If the plan and the product suit you, and the retail price is right, then it is up to you to decide if you want to get involved with the company.

The Step Plan

Let's look first at a simple version of a *Step Plan,* and see how it works. Once you can understand this, then the more complex plans will make more sense to you.

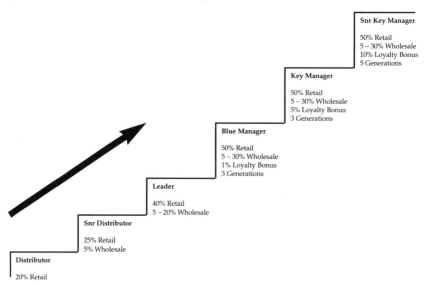

The basic Step Plan has every one starting at a pre-determined amount of commission. The more you sell, the higher the commission earned because the plan is based on volume of sales. It is important to note that this example of a Step Plan is very basic, and the titles used for the different levels will vary between companies. Several plans you may come across are likely to be more detailed than this example.

The commission that is earned is called your *Retail Profit* and is the difference between what you buy the products for from the company, to what you retail the product for to your customer.

Some plans have your commission on a *Sliding Scale*, and this quite simply is a scale that up to a certain amount of sales, usually when you *Breakaway* (achieve the same level as your sponsor) from your sponsor, your commission amount will vary. This variance will be on a monthly basis, but never returns to the original amount of commission that you earned.

Sliding Scale Plan:

Volume		Commission/Profit	Wholesale Profit
0 – 200	20%	Commission – Retail	
201 – 399	25%	Commission – Retail	5% Wholesale Profit
– –			
400 – 999	35%	Commission – Retail	15% Wholesale Profit
1000 – 1999	40%	Commission – Retail	20% Wholesale Profit
2000 – over	50%	Commission – Retail	30% Wholesale Profit

The example above highlights a very simple sliding scale. It is important to remember that for the purpose of these examples we have used as basic an example as we possibly can. Most plans that you will come across are likely to be far more sophisticated than this, and will warrant a detailed explanation.

The volume that is highlighted above the broken line denotes the monthly Personal Group Sales that you generate. When you are generating only £200 or less per month, your Retail Profit will be only 20%. You will not earn any *Wholesale Profit* from your distributors. Wholesale Profit is the difference between the sales between you and different members of your downline. When you are at a higher percentage of profit than they are, you may receive the difference either from the company, or, in same instances, the distributor will order the product from you and you will have the wholesale profit instantly. When you start to order in the next month, you will fall back to the 20% level.

When you achieve £201 in one month (this amount can be a single purchase, or an accumulation of purchases over the month from the company) you move to the next step up the ladder for commission. You are now on 25% Retail Profit, and you will enjoy the benefit of 5% Wholesale Profit generated from the sales of those people that you have introduced to the business and who have yet to achieve this level of sales production. At this point in time, your position is permanent, which means that the next month you will start at 25% discount, thus ensuring your Wholesale Profit.

When you have achieved over £2000 in any given month, your Retail Profit again is permanent. You will start the next month at 50% commission, or Retail Profit when you are selling the products to your customers.

If you were to achieve this position, then the following month order only £1400, you would still enjoy the 50% maximum discount. Some companies, however, will require you to achieve that particular amount of sales again in a calendar month on an annual basis. This is what is known as *'Requalifying'.*

Your reward for achieving a high volume of retail sales is a greater commission. Sometimes this can be as much as 50% greater than when you first purchased the product. This is a good reward system, and encourages the individual to generate a large amount of retail sales, and build a solid customer base.

From the customer base, you will sometimes find that the customer may have an interest in joining the company, and also benefiting from the discount available on products. This is a good sign, and you should encourage your customers to also market the products in the same manner that you are. You in turn will then earn a *Wholesale Profit* from these distributors.

In simple terms, if you are at a higher level of commission than this distributor, you get the Wholesale Profit of the difference between the two commissions.

It is worth noting at this point that you should be interested in having more than one distributor in your organisation so that the volume that is created is greater, thus ensuring you have a greater potential for income, but also just in case someone drops out, or for whatever reason has an off-month.

Royalty bonus

If the customer became a distributor, and then achieved a sufficiently high level of sales where they were at a Breakaway position, you then have a problem; they are on the same commission as you and therefore you are not in a position to earn any income. The Wholesale Profit that you previously enjoyed is not there. No need to worry; the company has overcome that by awarding a *'Royalty Bonus'* to you, based on the amount of personal or group sales that you have done in that current month. This phrase is sometimes called a Loyalty Bonus, Override or can sometimes be part of a Leadership reward plan.

Whatever it may be called in the company that you are with, or the company that you are looking at joining, it is the income paid by the company to you, when one of your distributors reaches the same level you are at and the Wholesale Profit stops.

Many people cannot understand that there is a higher income potential to be earned from a smaller percentage on this bonus scheme (because of the numbers in your network) rather than the larger Wholesale Profit amounts achievable before the distributor attained this higher level.

Invariably, it is better to receive a little of a lot, than receive a lot of a little. When someone is in this position within your organisation, it is likely that they are steadily recruiting and retailing the products, and they will be building their own organisation.

An example of income to be earned at the different levels:

£150 of products sold will generate	£30 Retail Profit (20% commission)

£200 of products sold second month	£50 Retail Profit (25% commission)
£100 sold by downline	£5 W P* (5% commission)

£1500 of products sold third month	£600 Retail Profit (40% commission)
£100 sold by downline	£20 W P* (20% commission)

£2500 of products sold fourth month	£1250 Retail Profit (50% commission)
£100 sold by downline	£30 W P* (30% commission)

W P* = Wholesale Profit

This chart does not take into account any payment of Loyalty Bonus (or similar name) earned from the sales of the downline.

You can see that there is money to be made by creating a large organisation, but it is important to be aware that hard work to build such an organisation is required.

We mentioned in our very first chapter that MLM and Direct Sales is not an industry to get involved in if you want 'to get rich quick'. It will take hard work, and a considerable amount of time to recruit, train and motivate your organisation to produce a high volume of sales.

You must also understand that you cannot receive the payments from the company if you do not generate the required amount of personal sales as set out by the company.

Where do you get the products?

In the marketing plan that you are looking at, if you are looking at a nationwide organisation, you need to be sure that the product delivery system meets your needs.

A large proportion of the companies in some parts of the world, S.E. Asia and USA, have appointed 'stockists' and their function is to act as a mini-warehouse. These individuals are trained by the company in Product Knowledge, and sometimes are distributors themselves within the company. You obtain your products from them, and they keep you informed of the new products being launched, possible product campaigns and any deletions or back orders of product. Their role will be to supply you with product from a closer location as opposed to direct from the company, which may be some distance away from you. Their stocks are replenished by the company on a regular basis to try and ensure that there is always ample stock for the network.

If this situation exists within your company, you need to ask if there is the ability to ship product direct to one of your distributors, and if so, does it have to be in full cases/minimum shipments, etc. You may find the business is slower to get off the ground if you are dependent upon product being shipped to you, then you have to repackage and ship on to someone else in another part of the country. Also, the extra cost of shipping has to be borne by someone, and it is usually the customer who pays the extra price.

If your company does not have a stockist system in place, you still need to know if you can have products shipped direct to your downline, and whether you have to order items by the case.

Also, there are some plans in existence where there is an *'Order Direct'* system in place.

This can be ideal for you if you are doing a nationwide recruiting campaign. The benefit to this system is that the product never comes to you! All product is shipped direct to the distributor, and they pay the company direct. You then receive the commission payable to you direct from the company. Many companies are using this system and find that it is a major plus for them when potential distributors are looking for the ideal company to join.

In the past, when many companies had a system in place where you ordered from your sponsor, it led to abuse by people who never paid for the products, or there were problems with the funds. This would usually mean a delay in either shipping the product, or the sponsor receiving the funds. If the funds were not forthcoming, it could sometimes mean that the sponsor was unable to order for themselves or other distributors in the organisation.

The Binary Plan

The Binary Plan can be summed up as a glorified Matrix Plan. The only true winners with this new scheme are the companies who adopt this marketing plan.

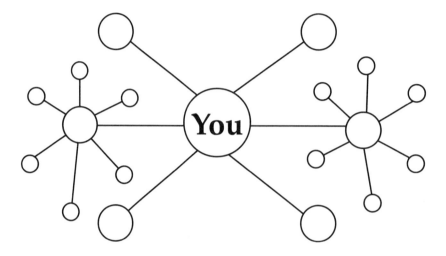

Recently we came across an American MLM company in the UK who had adopted this plan, and after speaking to a number of distributors, we were able to determine exactly how the plan really worked.

Again, it is important to mention that not all Binary Plans will follow this plan exactly, but this plan does appear to be fairly straightforward.

You as the recruit will be paid a 'bonus' when you have placed an equal number of recruits on either side of you. For the purposes of this exercise, we will put three on your left, and three on your right. The people that are recruited on either of your sides can have more than one place, and in order to do this, they can for a price, 'buy' their spots. When you have recruited your six members, there will be a payout for you.

When each of the six people duplicate what you have done, they too will receive a payout. When all six members have recruited their six members, then you will receive an additional bonus.

Some companies will pay the bonus out weekly, and this gesture is really an enticement for someone to invest a large sum of money in the hope of obtaining a quick payout.

Don't get us wrong; it is possible to make a considerable amount of money with this plan, but it is solely dependent upon you 'selling' your spots quickly, and you obtaining your bonuses.

There are no levels in this scheme, but from what we have found, the products are generally overpriced, and we found that the literature is quite glossy, and expensive to purchase. Whilst it may be worth considering joining a company who provide this scheme, please 'do your homework' first!

The Matrix Plan

Finally, the *Matrix Plan* is the plan that has caused some controversy recently. Depending on who you speak to, the plan either benefits the company or the distributor. There are several variations of the matrix system, and if this happens to be a plan you are looking at, you need to know what happens to the 'holes' in the system when someone drops out.

What this means is that as you recruit and sponsor people, so do the people above and below you, but where this plan differs from a Step Plan is that the people just fill into a slot below you. So, rather than have your own downline that can distinctly be shown as yours, and the sponsorship flow goes back to you, the Matrix Plan has everyone who signs an application form fit in the next available slot.

If you were to chart this plan, all of the efforts of those above you will benefit you in your anticipated income to be earned. What are the pitfalls of this plan?

There are a few, and you need to be aware of them. We aim to cover some of the more obvious ones here, and the not so obvious, to again provide you with an insight as to the workings of the scheme.

The first one is what happens to the 'holes' when someone drops out. In some plans, if someone drops out before you fill in the spaces, you don't get a full payment. Also, in some plans the holes will be filled, but because of the continual 'hole filling' you rarely achieve the maximum potential payout.

In summary, a Matrix Plan limits your front line, those people that you personally sponsor – the Step Plan where there is a 'Breakaway' does not. A Matrix Plan is contrary to MLM philosophy because a person who is active and works hard to build a team of productive distributors, will be penalised by the fact that there are limits to potential growth of the business.

Training of the marketing plan

Each company will have a variation on the marketing plans we have outlined, and each plan will have some unique feature that the others do not have. It is important for a distributor to understand fully how the plan works, how to explain it in stages to a new recruit, and how to keep the explanation as simple as possible. With each marketing plan there will be ways that the plan can work to the advantage of the distributor.

The company should provide some form of training on the marketing plan, along with product training to assist you to progress with the company. The marketing plans of many companies are not easy to follow, and by merely drawing pictures in a career-manual-type publication with a vague explanation, is not sufficient information for the majority of people to use as a reference tool when explaining the plan to potential new recruits.

We have come across many people who have reached a senior level within a company, and the financial reward has been great, but these people could not tell you how their plan works. All they know is that they sell a lot of products, they recruit a lot of people, and every month they get a substantial cheque paid to them.

This clearly is not the example to set to your new recruits, so it is important that the company you are looking at has a marketing plan that you can understand, and if you cannot understand the plan, there is training provided by someone who understands the plan, and is able to show others how the plan works to the best advantage of the distributor.

By understanding how the plan works, you can explain the plan in stages to your new recruits. You do not need to explain the entire plan to a brand new recruit. The best way for the recruit to learn is to give them a little bit at a time. Give enough information to get them to the first stage, and make sure they understand fully what is required of them. When that stage is reached, give them sufficient to get them to the next stage, and so on. This will ensure that the recruit gets the necessary training in stages, and by reaching the next stage, the recruit should be able to show that they have an understanding of the plan.

If you teach the plan in stages, you will not overwhelm the recruit and cause them to quit because they think it will be too hard. Also, by teaching the plan in stages, you can ensure that there is a solid foundation being built, and in the long term this should increase your chances for good financial rewards.

Not everyone who gets involved in an MLM or Direct Sales company wants to reach the highest level, or even wants to build an organisation with distributors scattered everywhere. Some people just want to sell a little bit of the product for a bit of extra cash. There is nothing wrong with these people, and you should make sure that you have people like this in your organisation.

Why? The reason you need people like this has been explained earlier within this book, but for the benefit of those readers who have skipped to this chapter, these people will never do tremendous sales figures, some may never reach the Breakaway point where they become independent, but they will always be there generating some of your group wholesale volume on a regular basis. Whichever company you are looking at the company will require a set amount of sales by you each month in order for you to obtain any form of Loyalty Bonus. This is a requirement by law, and you have two options – do the sales yourself, or recruit an organisation to do it for you. It is easier and potentially far more financially rewarding to do the latter.

Just think, you need to generate enough sales each month in order to qualify for your loyalty payment, you need to recruit, and you need to have your personal time. How are you going to do all of that each month? The answer is have lots of 'small' distributors that are not going anywhere, and use their volume to form part of your wholesale group volume.

Like all training, it will only be useful to you if you put into place what you have learned. Ideally, what you have been taught by the company you should be relaying to your distributors in stages, and talking to them regularly to make sure that they know how the plan will work best for them.

Pyramid Selling Act

The Pyramid Selling Schemes Regulations 1989 came into effect in the UK on March 1, 1990, and has been enforced in most countries throughout the world in modified form of one sort or another over recent years. The interpretation of the regulation is that 'selling schemes' shall be required to follow the guidelines as set out, and that the company and the individual are required to adhere to the regulations.

Within the limited space available within this book, we intend to provide you with a guideline to the different regulations relating to the Act and, we stress, this is to be taken only as a guideline. You are advised to check the specific laws relevant to your particular country as these are likely to vary from those shown opposite.

Very briefly:

- There is a limit to the amount of money you can invest for product from a Multi-Level Marketing company within a certain time-frame. This is basically your 'cooling off' period.

- There must be some written warning on the contract that states the income that can be derived from the business is dependent upon the efforts of the individual, and are not guaranteed.

- The company must accept the return of goods, provided they are in a 'saleable' condition if the distributor should decide to terminate his agreement. A handling charge shall apply for the administration required.

- There should be a warning that any individual seeking to become a distributor for the company should first seek legal advice.

- In order to receive commissions, royalties, etc. the sponsor must first be achieving the minimum required personal or group sales.

- The regulations also prohibit the acceptance of payments for training facilities unless it is made clear that the participant has a free choice whether or not to use the facilities and the charge is clearly stated.

There are other sections contained in the UK version of this document, but we have highlighted the key points here that each individual should be aware of before they enter into any agreement. In view of the international application of this book, we strongly recommend you obtain a copy, or refer to a copy, of the equivalent Act in force which relates to your particular country.

So you have decided to join – what's next? Please read on and discover for yourself just how to get started...

Learning Points From Chapter Two:

1. Do I know how the company I have chosen pays the distributors?

2. How competitive are the products that are offered by the company?

3. I understand how the various types of marketing plans operate, and I fully understand the plan from my company.

4. There may be legal requirements as to how I run my business, and I fully understand what they are and follow them and ensure my network do the same.

5. I have passed all of this information to the members of my network, and I have made sure that the network understands the marketing plan.

Notes:

_____

_____

_____

Chapter Three

Getting Started

The idea behind this chapter is to provide you with a clear guide, on a step by step basis, how to achieve success within the Direct Sales and MLM industries. How great the success will become is only dependent on one thing – *you!*

The beauty of this business is that anyone can succeed, anyone that is who apply themselves and are committed to improving their own lifestyle/health/finances/family's future. We wonder how many of you started with your present company for one or more of these reasons.

Has it been achieved yet??

Possibly not yet in the way you wish for. This is where the 'Getting Started' chapter will go a long way towards achieving a clearer indication of the direction you should take and the activities you need to complete when joining an MLM or Direct Sales company. By ensuring you follow the 'Stepping Stones to Success' (Chapter Four) this will help you along the path to your own success.

What we will be looking at first is how to get you started and how to raise the level from where you are now and build on your existing successes, thus enabling you to step up to the next level, and then the next, and then the next!

Not everyone wants extra money/cash, do they? A few people just need something to get them out of the house to meet other people, or perhaps they feel bored in their current full-time job. Whatever the reason, this business is likely to achieve a far higher income producing potential than anything they have done before. As you will discover, in most cases the start-up costs can be very low when compared to other industries. Invariably you will have no need to buy a shop/premises or pay exorbitant fees for a franchise and thereby initially get deeper into debt. Yet the returns you can achieve are massive and the satisfaction overwhelming – if you work smartly and follow the guidelines contained within this book.

Whichever company you choose to work for will either have products or services (or both) to sell, and as a result you will need a certain amount of product training if you are to acquire suffi-cient knowledge about the respective products to promote and sell them.

Product knowledge

Firstly, we mentioned earlier about using the products of your selected company. Do *you* use the products? We hope so. It's *very* important to use the products yourself and in turn this will give you some experience of the benefits that can be obtained from using the products and it will provide you with your own 'story' (testimonials), and with these will come more knowledge – 'knowledge is power' as the saying goes, and in this respect it's true.

You need knowledge of the company, its products and the skills required to succeed. In connection with the products how much knowledge do you think it is necessary to have in order to sell them?

Whilst it's true to say that you will naturally need to possess some knowledge of the various products available you do *not* have to be an expert! What is required is the 'essential' pieces of product information which will lead to the products being sold – "What does it do for me?" This is the very question which we all ask when confronted with a buying decision: "What does it do for me?"

It may be that the slimming formula is unique in certain ways chemically. Most customers will not be too interested in the chemical formula because it will mean nothing to them. However, when shown *how* the product can assist in weight reduction and given examples (pictorially) of the effects – these are known as the *benefits* of the product – most people wishing to source such a product will be interested and will be more inclined to buy.

This is true of virtually all products, whether it's a slimming product or a range of skin care or cosmetics. All that is needed is to find the customer's 'needs and/or wants' and present the relevant product's best features as *benefits* to a particular customer and they will buy!

As we stated earlier, knowledge of the products is important but *more* important is the *skills* required to 'sell' them. Selling products generally means 10% knowledge and 90% skill application, although you should know 100% of the 10% to inspire confidence (both for you and in you).

There will be *very few* customers who want to know extensive technical detail about the product or service, and they are *very* few, possibly as low as one in two-hundred-and-fifty. And each time you talk and read about the product you will be extending your own knowledge and confidence.

Finally, the dangers of trying to be solely focused on the technical aspects of the product and becoming a 'guru' on all the products available could mean that when you are talking to a potential customer and explaining in minute detail all of the associated features of the product or service they get 'blinded by science' and don't buy because you didn't cover the 'what does it do for me?' question (benefit). Or in the event you are talking to a potential new recruit and explaining the product range of your company they may feel intimidated by your extensive (and unnecessary) level of product knowledge and feel they could never achieve your high level of knowledge and therefore will not join.

The bad news is they may be employed by Sony or Kodak (or another large organisation) with over three thousand staff and you've just lost a potentially massive customer base and distributor network. What if... their brother was employed by another large company or they tell a friend how technical you have to be to work for *your company* and they also work for a large multinational organisation, you could lose them too – bad news, eh?

Hopefully you will have learned that you do *not* need to be an 'expert' on product knowledge but that it's essential to develop the 'skills' of selling – what is known as 'people skills'. In addition you will need to apply the skills of storytelling – by creating *drama!*

It is true to say that – **'Facts Tell But Stories Sell'.**

Your positive stories (testimonials) about the products or services are very important in the course of the sales process and so are the stories of your network. You will be building a picture in the mind of the customer of the many benefits derived from your product and to do this effectively requires skill with your storytelling. Be honest, sincere and dramatic! Ensure you practise telling your stories as often as you can to establish your own confidence and competence. Remember you may need to borrow stories from your upline and their customers in the early days. This is important because you will not be able to cover all the products with testimonials initially, but it is highly likely that your upline can.

To acquire these skills will for some, be a very small step, but for others it will be a big 'leap of faith!' By this we mean that certain people may feel they did not consider joining this company to 'sell'. If they had known it involved selling they might never have joined.

Well, to be fair, life is all about selling; from a very early age we *all* learn to sell. Children learn how to 'sell' first. The little five-year-old boy asking his dad for an ice cream says "I want an ice cream!" He will start having a tantrum and become very upset when his dad says "No!" Ultimately he will *not* get the ice cream.

However, the little girl learns from a very early age how to sell her story and she will curl up to her dad and say something like "Daadddy, can I please have an ice creammmm, daadddy (kissey kissey)?" Inevitably the father will give in to such tactics, such is the power of the female and more particularly the 'selling technique' utilised. How many of us have been caught by this ploy?

So if life, in this context, *is* all about selling (in one form or another) what else can we offer you to ensure you achieve a good start with your chosen company? One method of building a plan for success is to identify how many products or services you need to sell in order to achieve your target figure. The target figure may have been selected because this is your own personal figure of sales required in order to generate sufficient commission, bonuses or profit! Or the target could be one set by the company in order for you to attain the next qualifying level; either way it is likely to be the 'minimum' you need to achieve in a given period. An example might show that when you have done your calculations you have established that you need to sell the following each week:

- One set of skin care programme
- Two bottles of 50ml perfume
- One weight-loss programme
- Two items of household cleaner

the sales of which will provide you with sufficient money to meet your objectives or to achieve the company's target. It may be that you actually need to sell more than this example shows (or less) but once you know what your minimum requirements are you are much more likely to be able to achieve them.

This is part of having an 'Objective'. Please allow us a moment to digress. You may have read the children's classic *Alice in Wonderland* which included a paragraph something along these lines:

As Alice approached a cross-roads she noticed there were roads going off in many different directions and she was unsure about which road to take. Sat beside the cross-roads was a small animal character whom she asked "Which way should I go?" The animal answered "Which way do you want to go?" Whereupon Alice replied "I don't really care!" In response to this the animal character stated "Then it doesn't much matter which way you go, does it?"

The moral here is that if you do not have an objective or more specifically a 'direction' of where you want to be, it will be almost impossible for you to get there. We have a useful phrase for you to remember:

If you don't know where you're going, how are you going to know when you get there?

We could write many chapters on this subject alone and we are sure that other writers will also have done the same, but for now just remember that to succeed in any role you should have an objective and this objective, whilst being achievable and attainable, must lead you towards the direction you wish to go – with your business, your ambitions and your life.

Essentially, when you get started with your chosen company there will be much to learn and take in and sometimes it may seem like too much. You will have some adjustments to make in the way you digest all the information, both product knowledge and skills knowledge, but once you begin you will quickly realise that it will definitely all be well worth the effort. But before you can really start on the road to success you need to develop a track to run on... not a route cast in stone but a track you can build on and develop, an effective tool for the job to ensure success is within your grasp, and we have provided such a mechanism within this book – something you can constantly refer to whilst you travel along the road to success.

This will be part of a much bigger process in the environment of selling products and services and we shall enlighten you further on the subject of selling in what we have entitled the Stepping Stones To Success...

Learning Points From Chapter Three:

1. I use the products regularly, and I ensure that the various members of my network do the same.

2. From using the products available from the company, I have started to compile my own story of my results and/or income.

3. I have taken the time to determine what I want to achieve by joining the company, and I have written these objectives down and regularly refer to them.

4. I know who my sponsor is, and I regularly keep in contact to learn more about the company and the products.

Notes:

_____

_____

_____

_____

Chapter Four

Stepping Stones To Success

There are many ways to promote and sell your products or services, although what may work in one town or country will not necessarily work in another. The methods used to sell cosmetics in Malaysia may differ slightly from those used to sell the same products in England. And similarly, the methods used to sell specific services like insurance in Germany will differ from those used in Canada. However, although the actual methods and associated advertising may vary to take into account the local culture, population requirements and legislation, the basic principles of selling will always apply. This leads us into what is known as the Sales Process…

The Sales Process

This is such a wide, even vast, subject that many books have been written solely on this subject alone. However, we aim to provide for you here a brief guide to the key elements involved with the Sales Process and how you can benefit enormously by following the tried and tested stages used. Occasionally you will find the process is reduced or even extended to accommodate a certain company's culture but essentially it follows a standardised format across all industries.

The Sales Process in one form or another will be familiar to you when related to everyday situations, when you go shopping for a certain item of, say, clothing. When the friendly assistant greets you they are likely to ask a few pertinent questions relating specifically to your actual requirements. From the answers they receive they will show you the item, perhaps a jacket/suit/blouse, and you like it (you are interested); it may be the style, colour or price which attracts you but at the end of the day you're interested. The 'trained' sales assistant will allow you to 'try on' the article of clothing (you are now entering into the 'ownership' phase) and is likely to sincerely compliment you on how good it looks/fits, etc. The untrained staff will be uninterested in you or the product and therefore unsuccessful in making a sale, ultimately allowing you to walk out whilst they finish their conversation with someone else!!

You may well get a good feeling about the clothing you are trying on but be unsure about purchasing it due to:

    A. wanting a 'second' opinion
    B. the style (is it you?)
    C. cost

The ever skilled assistant will then describe some of the features of the clothing (product) like its permanent crease, the fact that it's easy-clean and the height of fashion. Along with these will be the accompanying benefit statements: the permanent crease means that you will never have to worry about the look of the clothing for it will always retain its 'just pressed' image, or the fabric is made of an easy-to-clean washable material and therefore this means you will not have expensive laundry or cleaning bills. It is unquestionably these benefit statements (what it will do for the customer) which close the sale every time.

The result of this clarification and confirmation of your 'feelings' and desires about the product and the subsequent explanation of the benefits will ensure that you will not want a second opinion for the salesperson has already supplied one, and the issue of style will also be met by the reassuring and sincere salesperson. Finally the matter of cost will be overcome by making comparisons with the value for money on offer, the latest sale prices or explaining the benefits of the company's finance arrangements. Ultimately you will be dealing with this sort of objection much as you would deal with any objection and we shall discuss this topic later within this chapter.

As stated several times now, it is the benefit statements which will sell your products or services – answering the customer's question of "What will it do for me?" – with *your* company's range of products the same sort of benefit statements can be utilised although you will need to give it some thought – the moisturiser is made of XXX which means that your skin will always retain its naturally healthy tone and retain those youthful looks (and admiring glances!). You will need to practise this type of benefit statement with your colleagues, manager or recruiter, to ensure it relates directly to your particular company's product range and has the desired effect. Practice makes perfect so keep practising!

What we briefly experienced in the earlier example given above is a process whereby the effective salesperson has warmly greeted the customer and subsequently asked a few specific questions to elicit information relating to their requirements. After this the salesperson has moved to the next phase of the process and courteously showed the customer the item(s) or products, explaining the key features and the associated benefits for the customer. Finally the salesperson has 'asked for the order' or 'closed' and taken the money and issued a receipt. Along the way the salesperson may have needed to overcome objections or concerns raised by the customer, which is all part of the Sales Process. Ultimately by providing such high quality and attentive service the satisfied customer will not hesitate in returning to the salesperson for further orders in the future, and additionally will not hesitate to recommend the salesperson and company to their friends and family.

As stated above, this Sales Process applies across an extremely wide range of industries and product types. In one form or another it will certainly apply to all MLM and Direct Sales organisations; even though some companies do not physically 'show' the product, providing only a picture or a sample, you will discover this too can be overcome by following the Sales Process described below. By providing the sort of service consumers want you will find it much easier to sell the products they need and thereby increase your chances of success.

So let's break down the Sales Process into smaller sections to more closely consider the methods applied and see precisely what it is that you need to do to ensure your success;

i.   Preparation – know your product and the company
ii.   Greeting – warm and friendly
iii. Ask questions – open and closed
iv. Show product – describe features and encourage 'ownership'
v.   Explain benefits of product – answer the 'What will it do for me?'
vi. Overcome objections – feel, felt, found
vii. Ask for order – close
viii. Repeat Business – referrals

If we accept the Sales Process essentially forms several sections or parts then it is important to understand how each one is inter-linked with each other and how, when correctly applied, they follow a guaranteed route to success for the salesperson. So let's begin;

i. Preparation

Before you greet a customer there are certain things which you will need to familiarise yourself with and these will take the form of:

a.   the company
b.   the products
c.   the Sales Process

We have already talked about a) and b) earlier in this book and therefore we are now looking at the Sales Process. Part of this process takes into account your need to properly prepare yourself for the meetings with customers.

This means the mental approach to dealing with customers; knowing the questions you will need to ask of the customers in order to discover their needs and wants, ensuring you have the right attitude and motivation and ultimately preparing yourself to guide them towards the products you and your company have to offer. By compiling in advance a range of questions which are not asked as an 'interrogation' of the customer but more as a conversation, you will inevitably discover the sort of products and services which your company can offer the customer and therefore which the customer is likely to buy.

For the particular products available from your company this compilation can take some time to complete; therefore we suggest you shorten the time-frame by asking your manager, recruiter or sponsor for some assistance. You can also listen to other colleagues within your company and collect some useful tips as you go along – it may help to write them down as you hear them so as not to forget later. After a while you will have collated a number of useful questions and phrases which you can start to use, and measure their effectiveness. You should *not* read them from a 'script' when in front of the customer! With constant practice and familiarity the questions will become second nature and will sound more natural.

At the same time the 'preparation' phase will also allow you to collate a number of ways of dealing with objections should they arise (more on this later – Section vi).

By preparing yourself with the questions to ask the customer (and in the right manner) and by providing explanations of the company and the products and also being aware of the ways to overcome objections, you will arrive at the point of asking for the order – the Close. Some companies provide very good in-house training programmes on these areas but all of the following sections will cover these steps.

Another part of the preparation process which will benefit you to remember requires you to familiarise yourself with the various items of literature, brochures and samples available from the company. As you will discover, effectively utilising the company's literature is another way of increasing your chances for success.

Good preparation is important, but inevitably in whichever industry you are in, you will need to greet the customer, and in order to make the right impression, this requires other skills…

ii. Greeting

When meeting people, customers or business contacts, one of the first rules you need to ensure is:

'You make your first impression last!'

It does not matter whichever industry you are in within the sales environment you will need to greet the customer warmly and friendly. If it's your first meeting, not so friendly that you appear to have known them for twenty years but certainly sufficiently friendly enough to be well received by them. Be genuine and natural, but most of all, be sincere. Good, regular eye contact is important here to establish confidence and trust.

You will need to think carefully about the clothes you should wear for your meeting – this will depend to some extent on the people you will be in contact with – not too smart to appear over-dressed but at the same time not so casually dressed to appear scruffy and having made no effort at all. In addition your general appearance needs to be carefully checked; take a look in the mirror now and see if you meet the following criteria:

For Men:	clean shaven or 'tidy' beard
	neat or 'styled' haircut
	use aftershave or cologne
For Women:	neat hairstyle
	not too much make-up
	attention to eyes
For both:	clean hands and fingernails
	clean shoes
	clean and appropriate clothes
	use deodorant and/or cologne
	beware of bad breath

Personal hygiene is increasingly becoming a major factor in why people do (and do not) buy from sales staff. It has been known for agents/distributors who are demonstrating their products or services within a customer's property to lose potentially large orders because they had a personal hygiene problem – body odour, bad breath, etc. Perhaps you can recall the last time you were confronted by a salesperson who suffered from one of these ailments – how did you feel? And more importantly, did you buy? We suspect probably not. Check out how you meet the above areas and make any necessary adjustments immediately.

iii. Ask questions

In the example given earlier where you visit a retail store to look at items of clothing we suggested the most successful salesperson will have asked certain pertinent questions. To be successful in the sales industry you need to ask a mixture of different types of questions. Mainly these fall into two distinct types and are known as 'Open' and 'Closed' questions.

Closed

This type of question is important for extracting precise and often factual information from a customer and they usually generate a short one or two word or yes/no answer:

- Q. "Do you have a bank account?"   A. Yes
- Q. "When did you move here?"   A. Sept 6th
- Q. "Do you prefer the red or the green?"
  A. The red
- Q. "Is it convenient to speak to you now?"
  A. No
- Q. "How many can you afford?"   A. Seven

As you can see, the above closed questions allow the customer to give only a short or very specific answer. Whilst the information obtained can be very useful, and in fact is often essential, it forms only a small part of the overall 'picture' of the customer's situation or requirements. We need to work on fully completing this 'picture' by asking more questions.

Open

Therefore what is required are a range of questions which elicit more relevant and somewhat fundamental and emotional information from the customer, and that is their 'feelings' or desires. It is this sort of correctly worded question which allows the customer to open up to you and express their true feelings or desires about their requirements. It will also allow you to phrase suitable supplementary questions to clarify and quantify various aspects of their initial response. Please note the following examples of 'open' questions:

- Q. "How do you feel about the new range of products?"
  A. I quite like the texture of the skin care products in the range but I would like to see a larger selection of hair care products, especially for the darker hair type.
- Q. "Why have you purchased your current perfume?"
  A. Because I liked the fragrance and it was not too overpowering or expensive.
- Q. "Why is it important for you to secure a regular income in retirement?"
  A. It is very important, as I need to maintain our standard of living when we stop working as the bills will still need to be paid.

From these examples you will note the difference from the closed type of questions. With the above examples of open questions it can be seen how the customer is allowed, even encouraged, to provide a much more intensive and detailed response. The customer is provided with the opportunity to 'open up', and divulge very useful information about their particular feelings and desires about the subject-matter under discussion.

Open questions allow the customer to provide much more than just a one or two word answer as they are expressing their feelings, emotions, desires, wants and needs. And you will only truly know what they are and subsequently try and meet these requirements by asking appropriate open questions.

Ultimately what is required is a structured method to your presentation of the products, or the literature about the products, and this will be made easier if you have asked the correct questions in the early stages of the Sales Process and in addition, *listened* (which is as important) and acted upon the answers you receive. Too often sales people ask good questions and fail to properly 'listen' to the response from the customer. The consequence of which is they then proceed to offer the customer the incorrect product for their needs and wonder why they didn't buy it. Or they get confronted with a tirade of objections which they find difficult to overcome and subsequently fail to secure a sale.

We mentioned earlier "How hard do you want it to be?" and this could well be a classic case of someone not listening and reacting to the answers the customer provides and ultimately offering the wrong product or service, result – *no sale!* It is occasions such as these which make people disheartened and disillusioned with the sales role, but if only they had not made things so hard for themselves…

It needn't be that hard if you just follow these simple steps to success:

1. Ask a suitably worded question (open or closed)
2. *Listen* and if necessary take note (write down) of the answer
3. If required, ask another suitably worded question for clarification
4. *Listen* and take heed of the response
5. Act on the responses you receive – ensure your product/service matches the customers requirements

Perhaps a further example might help;

- Q. "From all of the products you've seen which one do you like best?"
  A. The XYZ hand cream.

- Q. "What are you looking for from this product?"
  A. I need a hand cream which can soften my skin and protect it at the same time.
- Q. "So if the XYZ hand cream could achieve this you would buy it?"
  A. Yes.
- Q. "I am pleased to tell you the XYZ hand cream will achieve the things you require and in addition it will also moisturise and prevent chapped dry skin. How many shall I order for you?"
  A. I'll take two tubes, please.

Okay, so the above example of questioning went all the way to the close but believe us that's how simple and how easy it can be if you follow these simple steps to success. Ask suitable open and closed questions, *listen* and act upon the responses you receive and select the most suitable product or service which meets the customer's requirements. "How hard do you want it to be?"

With practice you will discover how to use both open and closed questions in the right quantity and this is very important. Not too many closed questions so as to make it appear like an interrogation and not too many open questions which may prohibit you from obtaining the other important 'hard facts' or the yes/no type answer. Correctly applied the questioning skills are an extremely effective method of increasing your sales ability and ultimately are a necessary skill for developing your business.

Before we move on to the next stage we would like you to complete the questionnaire on the following page. By answering the questions as honestly as possible you will learn how effective your listening skills are and discover where you need to increase your powers of attentive listening.

There is no right or wrong answer to this questionnaire, just the one which you believe directly relates to the way you perceive a given situation or customer. So give the questionnaire a try, you may be surprised by what you learn!

Check out your listening skills

	Yes	No
1. I look at people when I listen to them		
2. I listen to people when I look at them		
3. I listen attentively to what people say		
4. I take notes to keep a record		
5. I am not easily distracted		
6. I ensure control is maintained in difficult situations		
7. I allow the customer to ask questions		
8. I do not cut in when they ask questions		
9. I am always 'there' when the customer speaks		
10. I present a smiling face even when they can't see it		
11. I always check their questions for clarification		
12. I always ask questions for additional clarification		
13. I do not attempt to dominate the conversation		
14. I do not force my beliefs on the customer		
15. I ensure the customer feels comfortable speaking		
16. I encourage open and controlled discussion		
17. I watch for non-verbal communication		
18. I regularly monitor the evident body language		
19. I passively listen to others present		
20. I want to improve my listening skills		

How did you score?

Before you see the chart overleaf for the answer, we wish to highlight question 9 which asks if you are 'there' when the customer is speaking.

This primarily means, you *must* be there both physically *and* mentally when in conversation with a customer. Too many sales-people mistakenly ask the customer questions whilst their own mind is somewhere else – thinking about last night, sports results, the family, tomorrow night, etc. – essentially, you *must* be 'there' with the customer to ensure you are attentively listening, paying attention and watching for the buying signals. More on these in the next chapter.

If you have ever experienced talking to someone and thinking 'they are not listening to me' you will know how it feels. Too many salespeople make the mistake of not focusing their own mind on the customer, and paying full attention to their needs and wants. As we shall learn, the customer is always king.

So here are the results for the questions:

Score
- 1 to 5   'Yes' answers – practise your listening skills; I said: *practice your listening skills*
- 6 to 10   'Yes' answers – room for some improvement, we think
- 11 to 15 'Yes' answers – quite good, keep practising though
- 16 to 20 'Yes' answers – you listen extremely well

For those of you who did not hear us the first time (!) listening skills are another part of the overall Sales Process which with practice will ensure you maximise the opportunities which will exist for you. Make sure you take advantage of these opportunities by listening attentively, actively and by being 'there'.

iv. Show product(s)

At this stage you will have identified one or more of your product range which is likely to meet with the requirements of the customer. It is possible that you have several products which could meet their requirements but it is down to you to use your skill to focus on the most *suitable* product(s) for this particular customer. If you are able to physically 'show' the product to the customer it will naturally help them with their buying decision but this is not always possible so alternative methods of promoting the products will need to be considered. This again is where literature, and more specifically 'Testimonials', will greatly assist in confirming to the customer the value and benefits to be derived from the products. The danger of showing the customer six, eight or fourteen different types of products all of which are very similar will be to provide too great a choice and ultimately result in confusing the customer where they will subsequently not buy anything!!

You ideally need a structured method to your presentation of the products and as discussed earlier this will be made easier if you have asked the correct questions in the early stages of the Sales Process. However, on the basis you physically have a small selection of products short-listed for the customer to peruse, and if you haven't done so already, pass these products to the customer to let them handle them, touch them and if possible, use them. If the product is a perfume or hand cream this is easy to arrange and they should certainly be encouraged to try them. If, however, the product is of a larger dimension or if you have only literature and brochures available, this may not entirely be possible.

Therefore alternative arrangements will need to be made for the customer to 'try it and see'. Remember the 'Testimonials' we mentioned earlier? This is an occasion where the agent/distributor uses his or her skills to create a scene or picture for the customer to imagine ownership and visualise the benefits.

If the customer wanted to buy a car, a test drive could be arranged very easily. If, however, the customer wanted to buy a savings policy you could not provide them with something to hold, or could you? We expect there will be examples of your company's past performance and although they do not guarantee future growth it can be taken as an example of the performance attained during a given period, which when compared with other similar companies will show comparative and measurable market performance – quite valuable for assisting in their decision-making process.

Naturally any product needs to be well presented. If boxed the box and packaging must be in good condition, if clothing they should be clean and crumple free to ensure they are shown at their best. If it's jewellery you will need to ensure it is clean and if possible have available some bright lights to show the reflections of the stones or gold. If you are using brochures or leaflets to promote the products ensure they are not marked or soiled in any way or have the remains of a coffee cup stain left on them. Good presentation of the products is *very* important to create the correct image and effectively generate the 'desire to own' in the customer.

By allowing the customer to touch, handle and try the product you are instilling into them the feelings of 'ownership'; sub-consciously they are weighing up in their mind the feeling of owning this particular product. How many of us have passed by a shop window and looked at a very expensive suit or coat and imagined ourself dressed in it? Or looked at a Ferrari and imagined ourself behind the wheel driving down the road?

Well, this physiological approach does work, and by allowing the customer to handle the products they are imagining themselves owning the product and this, if used effectively, will assist you tremendously in the selling process. However, you must pay attention to the customer during this phase because you need to observe their reaction to the product and its associated features as they start to handle it. Very quickly you may notice positive expressions and smiles coming from the customer, which is likely to indicate they like the product!

If you observe lots of frowning and glum looks from the customer this does not necessarily mean they do not like the product, only that something is on their mind (possibly not connected at all with the product – personal life for instance, missing their favourite TV programme or worrying about their children) – essentially it's up to you, the salesperson, to uncover these apparent concerns by asking appropriate questions to clarify. Do they relate to your product or service and if so deal with them as soon as possible so that you can overcome what may be a stumbling block to a successful sale.

More on this in Objection handling – Section vi.

While discussing the product and, where possible, allowing the customer to handle it and try it, you should be confirming the features of the product and these merits should be in keeping with the customer's previously disclosed requirements. To be the most successful at selling, the product must have some or all of the features they were looking for.

Whenever and wherever possible a demonstration is an extremely effective method of showing the products off. One of the big advantages of showing the product from an MLM or Direct Sales company is that invariably you will have a 'one on one' meeting with the customer thereby ensuring they get concentrated and focused attention, not part of the rush hour in a busy store. We shall look later at 'Party Plans' and the home market of demonstrating products. For now please accept that if the products are good, you have asked the correct questions and provided the customer with the most suitable product, if people can't try it or see it as theirs they might buy.

But if you have created a 'vision' of ownership and where possible allowed the customer to imagine and believe in the benefits available by purchasing the item, *if people **can** try it they will buy!*

v. Explain the benefits

Whilst good questioning (and listening) skills are important within the Sales Process so too is describing the features of the product or service. It is important for a customer to believe the product they are considering to buy has the associated features they had short-listed and maybe a few more they had not considered. But people do not buy the features a product or service offers, they in fact buy something very different, *they buy the **benefits!!***

Or more precisely, *what the product or service will do for them!!*

When you last bought a kettle did you buy it because it looked nice, it was the right colour to match with your kitchen or maybe it was because you recognised the brand name to be one of uncompromising good quality? Quite possibly all of these statements were part of why you bought the kettle you bought.

However, the *real* reason you bought the kettle, was because you 'needed' hot boiled water!!

The earlier statements were all 'features' of the product: colour, style, brand name. The reason any of us buy a kettle is to obtain hot boiled water and the other 'features' of the kettle will determine which kettle we actually end up buying. The 'what will it do for me?' comment is answered by the different features of each kettle we look at. One may be the wrong colour so it does nothing for you, another may be too expensive so whilst you may like it you cannot afford it so it does nothing for you. Finally, you will find a kettle which has all of the features you require and is affordable; the 'benefit' of buying this particular kettle is that it meets your requirements and satisfies your budget and this is why you will ultimately buy it. Another example from a salesperson's perspective may help:

Salesperson: "One of the features of this kettle is a six-cup capacity." What this means to you (the benefit) is that you will not have to keep refilling the kettle so often when making tea/coffee.

Salesperson: "Another feature of this kettle is the built-in filter system." What this means to you (the benefit) is that you will always obtain 'clean' hot water and not get bits of limescale floating in your tea/coffee.

Salesperson: "Finally, this kettle features the latest safety designed fitted plug." What this means to you is that you will not have to worry about trying to wire a plug and getting it wrong since the kettle has an approved fitted plug ready to use.

These are just a few examples of how a salesperson could describe the associated benefits of the particular features of a kettle. You could turn this approach quite effectively to your own company's products and with practice develop a benefit statement for everything you have available to sell. If you can do this exercise with everyday objects like kettles you can be sure the same principles will apply for other less common items like machinery, stationery and even savings policies. At the end of the day all you are doing is analysing the features of the product or service and turning these features into benefits for the customer – which is the reason they will buy the product. Remember, if you asked the customer the right questions at the outset you will know which features are likely to be of interest and can therefore easily relate the benefits of these to the customer.

Hopefully you will now try this exercise out with your products or services and discuss your answers with your colleagues, recruiter, sponsor or manager; again with practice you will be surprised how quickly this simple process will improve your sales performance figures and lead to even greater success.

vi. Overcoming objections

As you will have noticed by now, there is a logical sequence involved with the Sales Process, and whilst the next stage is effectively the 'close', firstly we need to take into account the possibility that certain customers, for whatever reason (and we shall consider these shortly), are not yet ready to buy your product or service. So what should you do and how do you deal with the situation?

Firstly we should state that there will be occasions when you are with a customer (or a group of potential customers) and the above Sales Process will not follow exactly to script – by this we mean the customer may not raise any objections at all because you have completed such a good presentation they actually do not have any! Well done. Naturally this is a situation all salespeople in whichever industry ideally want to find themselves in.

In such cases you should not pre-raise objections on behalf of the customer "…but you were meant to query why we only sell these in 50ml size!?" Or, "…I still have to inform you how our model compares to the competition!" If the customer does not raise any objections move on to the 'close'.

Remember the 'How hard can it be?' statement from earlier; well, this is an example of how *easy* it can be so don't make life hard for yourself.

Take the order and move on.

Objections are another part of the Sales Process and you need to accept they will arise from time to time. They should be regarded positively and treated promptly to ensure the customer does not establish too many negative thoughts about your product or service. However, generally even with the best of presentations there can be some queries raised, not necessarily 'objections' as such but for the sake of argument we shall call them objections here. Essentially these are areas relating to the product or service under discussion which you have not fully satisfied this particular customer on, and either they have raised the question or you have detected they are not fully convinced of the benefits of the product. So what should you do now?

Most salespeople in this situation will start to repeat time and again the many features of the product or service. They will expand great volumes of verbal dialogue expressing the endless features the product has without stopping for breath and when the customer still looks unconvinced, dismayed or even confused the salesperson does not give in. Here they resort to handing the product back to the customer again for them to see for themselves how the features of this product far exceed those of the closest competitor.

Still frustrated at the lack of commitment from the customer to buy the salesperson will fall back to their last line of defence – the 'special offer'!

Here they will tell the customer how by purchasing this product or service the customer will save lots of money and in fact be better off as this 'special offer' is not available anywhere else. Unfortunately the customer will still not buy the product and the salesperson gives in, admits defeat and leaves without the order.

Does this scenario sound familiar to you? What did they do wrong?

They apparently provided very attentive service to the customer, they may have shown the customer the product, allowed the customer to handle the product and informed them of the many features of the product. They may have asked open and closed questions along the way to confirm they were showing the customer the correct and most suitable product in the range. So why did the customer not buy? Have you spotted what was missing yet?

Yes – they did not express the *'benefits'* of the product to the customer, answering the 'What does it do for me?' question. All the while the salesperson is restating the features of the product they *must* reconfirm what the particular benefit of this feature is to the customer and how it fits in with their requirements, which will be known from the open and closed questions asked earlier in the meeting.

Another way of dealing with either real or perceived objections from customers is to pre-empt them in the first place. When you complete your presentation ask the customer straight out "Do you have any questions or concerns about the product or service we have discussed?" Here you are allowing them the opportunity to raise any issues or concerns they may have. However, be careful when using this technique as sometimes it can backfire and you may end up receiving a mass of questions you are not prepared for. To prevent this situation arising we covered this subject earlier in 'Preparation'.

Essentially when you receive an objection or more precisely, a question about the product or service, you should treat this in the following way to ensure it is satisfactorily dealt with:

- ☺ Acknowledge the objection
- ☺ Confirm your understanding of their objection
- ☺ Check for any other objections before moving on
- ☺ Address the objections (one at a time) in a positive manner
- ☺ Confirm the customer is satisfied and move on

The acronym created is 'ACCAC' and this may help to recall the correct basis for dealing with objections. Firstly *Acknowledge* there is a question about the product or service politely and sincerely; do not attempt to put the customer down or make them feel stupid for asking such a question. Next *Confirm* your understanding of the objection raised; too often a misunderstanding at this stage leads to confusion later and a dissatisfied customer. It is often worth taking time to *Check* if there are any other additional queries at this stage; this way you can deal with them all in one go, albeit one at a time. Again treat such objections or questions with alacrity and sincerity. Now you need to *Address* the objection, so answer as fully as possible but without going over the top; be clear and concise, and once completed *Confirm* the customer is satisfied with your answer before moving on. Quite often, once any objections have been satisfactorily dealt with it is a very good opportunity to move on to the close.

Invariably the objections raised will fall into one of three categories:

1. Misunderstanding
2. Imaginary
3. Real

The customer has misunderstood something which you have said or explained about the product or they have misunderstood what the item can or cannot do. Therefore, you need to practise your presentation skills to ensure you are clear and easily understood. It may be the objection is based on an imaginary belief "...but if I take these weight-loss drinks I will lose my sight", and these need to be overcome by sincere and focused explanation – possibly providing any documentary evidence available to support your claims.

Finally, the objection may in fact be real; here the customer has a genuine concern about the product or service and needs clarification on some aspect of it. This requires you to ask more of the open and closed questioning skills we discussed earlier to elicit from the customer the basis of their concern.

Quite often you will find the customer will be satisfied with a rational explanation and a useful tip to try is shown in the following example:

Customer: "I think the water-filter system you have demon-strated is too expensive."

Salesperson: "I understand how you *feel,* as other people have *felt* like that too, but what they've *found* is when you compare the cost of purchasing bottled water regularly, the longer term costs of the water filter are minimal and the benefits of the purer, cleaner and convenient water supplied, far outweigh the purchase price."

This type of answer is often used once you have clearly identified the real objection. The *'feel, felt, found'* statement can be applied to great effect and usually overcomes most types of objection, but again it needs practice to perfect it and, more importantly, to make it sound sincere for the customer. How about another example?

Customer: "Do I really need to buy the complete set of cosmetics?"

Salesperson: "I understand how you *feel,* as others have *felt* like that too, but what they've *found* is that when you use all of the products as they were created they complement each other and provide the optimum results for you, ultimately providing better value for money."

Again the 'feel, felt, found' statement is adapted to suit the situation and works very well, satisfying the customer's concerns and identifying some of the benefits available and thereby leading the way towards the close.

Another alternative example may be helpful – if cost was an issue for the customer you could relate the daily cost of the product(s) to everyday items like, say, cups of coffee. If you know they drink about eight to ten cups of coffee a day you again acknowledge and confirm their concern and overcome the objection with a statement like: "…buying these products equates to only two cups of coffee a day; if you can do without the extra coffee you can afford the product(s) and obtain all of the associated benefits, isn't that what you require?" thereby leading you straight into the close.

This exercise is designed to get the customer to put the issue of cost into perspective.

There are many different ways of handling objections but the most successful ones always meet the criteria of 'ACCAC' we discussed earlier:

- ✓ **Acknowledge**
- ✓ **Confirm**
- ✓ **Check**
- ✓ **Address**
- ✓ **Confirm**

All of these were discussed earlier and the actual process used to achieve these may vary slightly from industry to industry, but essentially if you follow these steps you can be sure of either resolving the objection (if that's what it really is) and this will lead to a sale, or you will identify for both you and the customer the outstanding issues/areas which still require clarification at (hopefully) a subsequent meeting. Thus the sale is still not lost!

You may be interested to know of some other methods of handling objections which have been tried over the years and proven to be much less successful than 'ACCAC' mentioned above, these are as follows:

- ❖ **Ignore them**
- ❖ **Refute them**
- ❖ **Argue**
- ❖ **Tell (only)**
- ❖ **Erase them**

The acronym attached to this can be seen to read 'IRATE' and this is inevitably how you will make your customers feel if you should consider treating them in any of these ways.

Generally you need to think carefully, or have your answer pre-prepared in advance (training!), before you start to react to an objection raised by a customer. Take a moment to reflect on the last time you had a customer leave dissatisfied; did you fall into any of the following traps?

Ignore

They are certainly *not* likely to buy from you if you choose to ignore any questions, concerns or issues (objections) they have with your product or service. Why should they? If you are inept enough to fail in answering what may be a simple query the customer will not build a good picture of you, your product/service or your company. So please do *not* ignore the 'objection' for if you do, you will miss a great opportunity to show your knowledge of either the product, the service or your company, and the many benefits the customer can derive from all three!!

By acknowledging the objection you will alert the customer to the fact that you are both confident in your product or service, and equally that you are competent to discuss matters which are of concern to them. Each of these factors is important from a psychological point of view when establishing yourself with the customer and creating both trust and positive lasting impressions.

Quite often customers will recall each question or query they raised which was not answered, and this together with any other concerns they may have will determine whether or not they are sufficiently convinced or satisfied to buy your product or service.

Refute

Many people have tried to refute an objection from a customer by ineffectively disputing the points or issues raised by the customer; this in turn inevitably ends up in the objection turning into an argument and for how to respond to this see the next section.

If you find a customer has an objection which you believe to be unfounded you will naturally feel obligated to correct the customer by informing them of what you believe to be the right information. If you can back this up with clear evidence, then you are correct to advise the customer of their 'misunderstanding' regarding the subject at issue.

However, you must not do this in such a way that the customer feels put down, belittled or made to feel small. The customer will understandably feel put out by such treatment and as a result will be unlikely to purchase anything. Let's face it, no-one wants to be treated in such a manner so why expect our customers to accept it? – they won't, you will lose them and someone else will gain. Remember, it is so much easier to lose customers than to gain them in the first place – 'How hard do you want it to be?' Well, if you mistreat customers in any of these situations it will ultimately result in lost sales and lost business and make it very hard indeed. Therefore, we recommend you don't do it!!

When dealing with a customer who takes an opposing point of view on something related to your product or service all you need to do is follow the steps mentioned earlier – ACCAC. This will allow the customer to make their point and also allow you to clarify, confirm and hopefully convince the customer that you are providing the 'correct' information in connection with the subject under discussion. A well-treated and satisfied customer may tell two or three friends of how well they were treated by a salesperson/company but a dissatisfied customer *will* tell dozens of people!!

Argue

If you enter into an argument with a customer there will only ever be one winner – and it will not be you! Arguments should be avoided at all costs for customers are much wiser than you may give them credit for. They are better informed now than they have ever been about the products available, their legal rights and the type of service which they expect to receive. To secure the loyalty of a customer you must first prove you are worth dealing with. Arguing with them is unlikely to achieve this.

There are many old sayings about dealing with a customer and to a large extent they remain true to this day. Here are a few to remind you:

- The customer is always right
- Always accommodate the customer
- Customers don't care how much you know, they just want to know how much you care
- Don't fight to win the sale to lose the customer

This last comment reminds me of the saying where 'You can win the battle and lose the war'. Clearly where a customer is concerned you may well make the sale but at what cost? You could just end up losing the customer (and many others besides) and the long-term business which this customer could have provided for you, all for the sake of a small short-term profit.

It is therefore desirable never to become embroiled in an argument with a customer over the product or service you are discussing no matter how strongly you believe in them, as the resultant loser, one way or another, will be you!

Believe us, arguments never really solve anything and only provide fuel for the mouths of those who remain dissatisfied, whilst those who thought they had won foolishly don't fully appreciate the loss they have incurred.

Tell (only)

Quite often when an objection is raised by a customer the salesperson will 'tell' the customer to listen to their answer and 'only' their answer. This effectively means the salesperson is not really dealing with the problem and working cohesively and empathetically towards resolving it; they merely insist the customer listens to them and 'does as they are told'. Unfortunately this system does not work too well in the modern world because the customer is much better informed these days, as mentioned earlier, and as such they expect to have their query explained and satisfactorily resolved, not brushed aside, and then be treated as someone without a brain because they were stupid enough to ask such a daft question!

An example may help:

Customer:	"Can you tell me why this model of watch has the extra set of hands on it?"

Salesperson:	"You mean you don't know!!! I thought everyone knew why these watches have extra hands on their face; you surprise me that someone of your calibre does not know. Okay, so I shall tell you. It comes down to the fact that the model of watch you are going to buy has not only a normal analogue face but it also has a built-in stop-watch facility, and this is what the extra hands are for."

In the above example the salesperson is not only 'telling' the customer about the watch but also treating the customer as if they did not have the capability to understand them anyway – very much an aggressive salesperson and basing their sales patter on the assumption the customer will be buying the watch. Not, we are afraid, without receiving from the salesperson a much better explanation than this and with a greater appreciation of people skills (more on this later). What has the salesperson missed?

To start with they have not truly acknowledged the query in the first place (rule number one) and they have certainly not confirmed or checked with the customer about their query (rules number 2 and 3). The explanation, such as it was, was brief and bordered on insulting.

Finally, having never really explained about the item being queried by the customer (the second set of hands) the salesperson completely missed the opportunity to sell the benefits of the item and any of the other associated features of the watch and, therefore, as you might imagine, did not make a sale.

Unfortunately, this type of objection handling (if you can call it that) is remarkably common, especially where lower-priced items are involved. However, even if the product is of a lower price or where the customer is unable to be convinced of its worth, this still does not remove the responsibility from the salesperson of providing a 'service' to the customer.

As one of the sayings mentioned earlier stated:

The customer is always right – (even when he's wrong!)

We have added the second section because there may be occasions where you just cannot satisfy your customer's requirements. No matter which approach you take it is not acceptable to the customer. Such occasions are likely to be extremely rare but if and when they do arise you should treat the occasion with dignity, patience and understanding thereby retaining your true professionalism, and realise that 'you can't win them all'.

Erase them

This is not a new way of disposing of customers who do not agree at the first opportunity to buy your products or services.

Sometimes you may have to work that little bit harder for the order than you had originally expected and in such cases overcoming a whole range of different types of objections; successfully completing the sale at the end of it will give you one of the most satisfying pleasures and mental rewards that money itself could not achieve.

Certain customers will raise the type of objection which some poorly trained salespeople will merely chose to erase from their memory; they delete it, cast it aside and never address it. We are not referring to the earlier option of ignoring the objection but more of erasing it from memory.

Here once again, the salesperson will be unsuccessful, because they fail to acknowledge it exists and therefore fail to address there could be a problem for the customer in understanding some aspect of the product or service under discussion.

Often the salesperson will deny an objection was raised, because they have erased it from memory, and the customer alone will be left to remind the salesperson of the objection raised and which as yet still remains unanswered. Pity the poor salesperson who now has to attempt to retrieve the situation from the brink of disaster; this will truly be an uphill struggle. 'How hard do you want it to be?'

All of which is a needless exercise for had they adopted the 'ACCAC' principle stated earlier the customer would long ago have been satisfied and assured and the matter would have been resolved before it could ever become a potential sale loser.

Objection handling should always be a positive process and you must not be dismayed or disheartened when you receive them, for the customer needs to obtain your assurance that the product or service they are considering buying will satisfy their needs, and if you completed the first stages of the Sales Process correctly you will minimise the chances of objections arising in the first place.

They do, however, provide an opportunity for you to show you know your product or service and can satisfy the customer's underlying concerns or queries about them thus resulting in a successful sale. Again, 'How hard do you want it to be?' If you deal with the customer correctly all the way through the Sales Process then objections are unlikely to arise; alternatively if you rush through the Sales Process and attempt to skip corners at every opportunity, then objections will be a natural stumbling block for you to face, encounter and overcome. So again, practise, practise, practise – how hard can it be?

Remember, human nature being what it is, a well-treated and satisfied customer *may* tell two or three friends of how well they were treated by a salesperson/company, but a dissatisfied customer *will* tell dozens of people!!

Practise the skilful way of dealing with objections and you will always enjoy satisfying endless numbers of eager customers.

vii.   **Ask for the Order &**
viii.   **Repeat Business**

All of the above areas are leading inexorably towards 'closing the sale'.

Once again, many books have been written on this subject alone and include a wide variety of solutions to what should be the penultimate step in the Sales Process. In view of the importance of this subject, and in obtaining Repeat Business, we have devoted the next chapter to what has been described as the simplest and yet often most anxious period, during the whole meeting with customers – asking for the order and also, obtaining Repeat Business. In addition to these topics we also cover the various ways of obtaining Referrals.

Let's remind ourselves of how you reached this point. You have completed your preparation, greeted the customers, asked open and closed questions and listened; quite possibly you may have shown the products or at least a selection of literature, and you have also explained the benefits and overcome any objections. Now is the Time to Close…

Learning Points From Chapter Four:

1.   I have read and understood how the Sales Process works, and I am actively following the process when I am recruiting and retailing the products from my company.

2.   I know the various types of questions to use, and I regularly practise the skill of questioning.

3.   I have made sure that I have a good supply of current company product literature, and when possible, I have products to show and demonstrate to customers.

4.   I understand the features of my products, and I am able to explain the benefits of the products to my customers.

5.   I am aware that I will get objections, and I understand how to overcome them.

6.   All the information in this chapter is passed on to my network so that they are able to successfully promote their business.

Notes:

_____

_____

_____

_____

_____

_____

_____

_____

_____

Chapter Five

Now Is The Time...

Ask for the order

In closing, *Timing is everything.* Although there are various methods of closing a deal precisely, *when* the close is applied is the crucial element. Of course price plays its part in the final negotiations, as does the quality of the product or service on offer. More importantly, across the world of selling the timing of the close on the customer has been identified as the 'key' factor in successful closing. Some salespeople fail because they try to close too soon and the customer leaves believing the salesperson to be far too pushy; others leave the close far too late, the customer leaves and the sale is lost due to apparently inept and unconscious sales staff.

Closing is probably the most important part of the sales process, but it is the one step that people either overlook in their rush to sell the product or service, or fear prohibits them from asking the customer for commitment. Either way, the salesperson and the customer both lose out. It is important to bear in mind that the Sales Process is not always a rational process, but can sometimes be an emotional process, which has the customer looking at wants rather than needs, and the salesperson possibly being irrational about the price of the product.

So how do you close and what is required? You will have noted from the whole Sales Process there is a logical sequence of events to guide you through what for some are the dangerous waters of selling – these are stepping stones if you will – and by treading on each stepping stone in turn you will reach the sanctuary of the sale and the satisfied customer.

Not just one satisfied customer, but hundreds, maybe thousands! On the basis you have followed these steps and have now arrived at one of the final stages, the close, we shall endeavour to guide you across safely and with confidence.

You get what you deserve! Don't over-complicate the close. Here are a few brief examples of how simple it can be; on a sale of products for a weight-loss or skin-care programme comments like "When would you like to start?" or "How would you like to pay?" are quite short and yet very effective.

Alternatively, if cost was an issue relate the cost of the product(s) to everyday items like say, cups of coffee – if you know they drink about eight to ten cups of coffee a day: "…buying these products equates to only two cups of coffee a day; if you can do without the extra coffee you can afford the product(s) and obtain the associated benefits!"

This exercise is designed to get the customer to put the cost into perspective. In a way it's like another variation on overcoming objections, but with the added bonus that it leads straight into the close.

It has already been stated there are many books on the subject of 'closing' and also books designed to motivate you whilst going through the process. We have not written this book solely based around these subjects. What we intend to provide here is a guide to the way through what for some is very often choppy and uncharted water, by providing you with a basic principle to apply when you reach the stage of 'asking for the order' and which have a proven record of success. When used correctly you will not be 'selling' as such but effectively guiding the customer into making a conscious and positive *buying* decision!

We mentioned that timing is probably the most important factor in closing and this is true. However, timing is part of a much bigger cycle in the closing process. As you will have read earlier, the salesperson must pay attention to the customer, be attentive, ask questions, listen carefully to the answers and act accordingly. During this process you will observe certain movements by the customer towards the product/service or brochure under discussion. These movements could well convey Buying Signals and it is a collection of such signals which will indicate to the more experienced salesperson the customer is 'interested' and *may* wish to buy. Indeed they may wish to buy but if you do not ask for the order how can the sale be completed? Some salespeople are too embarrassed to ask for the order, others just fear the dreaded 'no' and yet more are concerned about the effects of being rejected, again! Most of which comes down to a few things like: lack of experience, lack of product knowledge or simply a lack of confidence.

When a customer looks at a product in a brochure or actually holds your product and makes positive gestures towards it like "This is very good" or "I like the way the bottle is shaped" or "Is it really only that price?" these are all known as *Buying Signals,* an indication the customer likes the product. At this point you could make what is known as a 'trial close' by stating to the customer: "Yes, it is *very* good and we have them available from stock. How many would you like?" or "I agree the bottle does have a very unique shape and is of a very high quality. How many were you thinking of buying?" or "It is amazing how they can produce it for such a keen price. How many would you like?"

In each example the salesperson has listened to what the customer has said and responded with a positive 'trial close' which invites the customer to buy the product. Quite possibly the customer may not buy so easily but if you do not ask for the order in the first place you are unlikely to get it. Therefore the trial close is attempted to see if the customer is ready to buy. If they are and the sale completes, great! If they are not ready to buy yet it is possible they still need convincing of the product's suitability for their needs or wants.

As described earlier, a few more questions may be appropriate or further explanation of the features and associated benefits may be required; along the way further trial closes will be applied to test the water, as it were, and see if the customer is now ready to buy. At this point it is possible you will obtain an objection or two and these need to be handled and dealt with as previously described. In this way you will overcome them satisfactorily and be in a stronger position to move towards the close.

The trial close, when used correctly, can be a very effective method of closing the sale much earlier than would otherwise have been the case and allows both the customer and the salesperson to resolve the issue about whether or not the sale can go ahead. Finally if the trial closes have failed to secure the sale the actual close itself will need to be applied and this can vary tremendously from industry to industry. It requires an application of people skills, customer knowledge, product knowledge and also timing to apply successfully.

Again we must assume for the purposes of this book that the salesperson has asked relevant and pertinent questions along the way in addition to attempting the trial closes mentioned earlier before reaching this stage. By conducting this process the salesperson will establish other factors relevant to the successful close and that is the areas of concern the customer may have expressed during the trial close period and the specific areas of need and want relevant to this particular customer. All of this 'evidence' collected along the way will benefit the salesperson in compiling their close. As such the close may simply be a question of asking!

Please note the following examples:

- "When do you want the {product} delivered?"
- "How many months' supply of the {product} do you require?"
- "If I can arrange for the {product} to be installed on Thursday morning will you be in?"
- "Do you want to pay by cash, cheque or credit card?"

The above 'closes' are all straight requests for the order, if somewhat assumptive, and allows the customer very little room to escape. Just complete the paperwork and thank the customer for their order. However, occasionally you will need to adopt a slightly different closing technique, one that offers the customer an alternative:

- "Do you want the {product} delivered on Thursday morning or Friday afternoon?"
- "Do you need one month or three months' supply of the {product}?"

- "Do you prefer to take the 50ml or 100ml size?"
- "Would you like the {product} in the satin or matt finish?"
- "How soon do you want to start on the programme, the first or fifteenth of the month?"

Essentially these questions are known as the 'alternative close' as you are providing the customer with an 'alternative' – it does not matter to you which one they take but they *will* be taking one or the other – a choice, yes, and a sale, most definitely! In amongst the above examples is a certain amount of assumption, that is you are assuming the customer will buy something; it just needs to be decided which colour, size, finish, model or method of payment is going to be chosen. This 'assumptive close' is also a very effective method of closing and as you have observed above can easily be wrapped around an 'alternative' or direct close.

There is nothing wrong with assuming the customer will buy your product or service, and this positive attitude certainly helps achieve a sale more often than not. But be careful that you are not drawn into always obviously assuming the customer will buy without first having gone through the Sales Process outlined above. Unfortunately some salespeople we have had to retrain have fallen into the trap of not only assuming customers will buy but they will buy whether or not the salesperson bothers to complete the Sales Process. This, of course, is not the case and in fact such salespeople invariably get caught out by a reduction in the sales they make and an increase in the number of people who dislike their sales methods. They are no longer following the Sales Process correctly, just interpreting it for their own purpose and cutting corners where they see fit. Naturally it will not work effectively under these conditions, although initially they might think it will. Eventually the resultant loss in business and income will catch up with them and guess who will be the loser!

We have worked hard on producing an effective acronym to use when salespeople are using the Sales Process, remembering that they do not just have to work harder to achieve their goals but also they need to work **SMARTER**.

In order to help the salesperson, whether they are at the earliest stages of selling or if they are experienced sales staff with many years in the industry, it is naturally important to remember the various stages of the Sales Process, and the following acronym will assist in this; you can then look at the best way forward for you.

Essentially you need to work **S.M.A.R.T.E.R.** not just harder:

S kills   All of the skills including questioning, demonstrating, benefit statements, people and closing skills have to be taught/learned, and *practice* is important. Practice. How many people remember their first failed transaction? Do you know why it failed? Did you learn from it? Have you done it again? Have you received any training or support on how to improve?

        Do you drive a car, because this practice relates to driving lessons – what would have happened if you had received no lessons? Would you have been able to pass your driving test? Without suitable lessons, would there be more accidents, and as a consequence, higher insurance premiums? *Yes!*

        Effectively utilising the Sales Process as outlined earlier, where questioning, listening and promoting the benefits to the customer is a guaranteed path to success also requires you to practise these skills. Unfortunately, many salespeople have difficulty at 'the close' because they have not correctly followed the Sales Process.

        When this process is followed, a successful close is almost guaranteed.

M onitor   Observe. Watch and listen for buying signals. Comments of "I like that" and "This is very good" are quite strong buying signals. Remember at all times to use your eyes and ears. If the customer is showing interest in the product or service, take the time to note what they like, and be able to summarise the positives. Sometimes the buying signals are not verbal – maybe just a nod of the head, or even the customer having another closer look at the product or brochure. When buying signals occur, ask a closing question, assuming that the buyer will go ahead, e.g. "Which colour would you like, the red or the blue?" Or, "Which size would you prefer – the 50ml or the 100ml?"

If you are not sure of a buying signal, you can take the time to reaffirm to the customer the benefits that the product or service has that match his needs/wants. "You stated earlier on, Mrs Customer, that you needed a 10ml size roll-on perfume with a high quality fragrance and a competitive price; as you have found this product exactly meets those requirements I can arrange to have this and the other products you wish to buy delivered tomorrow". Alternatively, "If I include the 10ml roll-on perfume together with the deodorant stick and the *eau de toilette* for the special price of XX would you go ahead with the purchase?"

As mentioned earlier, this type of 'close' is known as the 'alternative close' as you are giving the customer the option to take one or the other and not allowing them the choice of saying no! All you expect or assume is the answer will be yes, and the only issue is which one of the products will they buy.

Attitude Be positive, not pushy. You must remember that the customers are likely to spend a considerable amount of money on some products and they want to make sure they will like them. It is essential to focus on the 'positives' (benefits) relating to the product or service to ensure the customer does not overlook any of them. By maintaining a positive approach to the customer this will help overcome any doubts they may have. If the customer is showing interest in the product or service, but is indecisive on buying, this is not the time to push them. What should be done at this point is to identify their concerns (as explained earlier), highlight the benefits and match them to their wants and needs. If you had not been listening and observing the customer, do you think you could be able to satisfactorily complete this? This healthy and positive attitude should also follow on with each new customer and not just be reserved for a particular individual. Remember to keep a positive outlook.

You must appear organised and confident in your approach during the entire process, for this in turn will assist in obtaining increased sales.

R **ealistic**   Always remain realistic and truthful when discussing the product, as it will benefit no-one long-term if you are found to be 'stretching the truth' about what a product or service will or will not do. Remember we are expecting you to observe a certain code of conduct and this entails working to predefined ethics.

As such you will need to be approaching whiter than white when discussing your company and its products or services.

On occasions, a few salespeople will intentionally tell a customer incorrect information about the product or service they sell in order to secure an order. Unfortunately this is very short-term thinking because inevitably they will be found out, not today perhaps or even tomorrow, but they *will* be found out and when they are their career could be over! Of course it may just result in the loss of future potential sales in view of the 'trust' being lost by existing customers and also the loss of sales to their friends and acquaintances. Alternatively it may lead to severe disciplinary action being taken by the company concerned or it could mean, in extreme cases, the police becoming involved with their own investigation and a prison sentence beckons. Either way the consequences are likely to be significant and therefore we strongly advise against misleading the customer for personal gain.

Also under the heading of *realistic* you should consider the following;

Ability – Can the customer afford to buy your product or service? (We are not suggesting you prejudge their ability to pay, but for larger ticket items this may be something you need to consider very strongly and clarify before you invest too much time). If finance is required where is it coming from and how dependable is it?

Needs – This relates to your questioning skills. Have you asked enough questions? Have you been able to separate the needs and wants? Is the customer being 'realistic' about their proposed purchase?

This relates to how well you 'know your customer' – the better you know them the greater the opportunity to sell them something which is suitable and which will satisfy them.

Timing   Essential. More sales are lost because the salesperson jumped in too soon to ask for the sale, or waited so long the customer went elsewhere. This relates to experience, and is effectively another skill which can only be developed with practice.

There are many occasions which have been identified as *not* to be the best time for closing, and here are a few: when the customer is dissatisfied with the product or service, when the customer has not had his objections satisfactorily answered, when there are issues relating to cost and quality which again have not been satisfied or, quite simply, when you need to have both partners present for the decision and only one is in attendance.

To increase your chances of success with closing and to enhance your skills, you should ensure that you are attentive by watching and listening to your customer(s). From this you can judge the best time to close. Attempt the sort of trial closes mentioned earlier as this can bring forward the close, and after having satisfactorily answered an objection is also a good time to close. Remember you are trying to collect lots of 'yes's from the customers – they do like the product (yes) and they can afford it (yes) and they would like it delivered in time for a special event (yes), etc., etc.

At some point you need to have collected enough 'yes's to attempt a close. If the customer is holding the product and is showing a high level of interest, close there and then rather than wait until later. Take the time to get to know your customers as this will assist greatly in correctly judging the right time to attempt your close.

Experience   Can't be bought. The Sales Process is a proven and yet perpetual learning process. We should all learn from our mistakes, and if our attitude is positive, and we can analyse our mistakes to make the necessary corrections, we will continue to learn and develop our skills. This leads to continual professional development, but naturally takes time to establish.

Experience comes from watching and doing, so make sure you watch your counterparts and do as much and as often as possible. This will ensure you take on board some of the many skills required to succeed in the role and hopefully learn to avoid the elements which ultimately lead to failure.

Records   Do you keep records of the sales which you have made? We expect so, and we hope so, but if you don't then think again. Records can be an extremely effective method of obtaining Repeat Business and Referrals (more on this shortly). Assuming you do keep records, how effective are they? How do you monitor how well you are doing? How can you improve on something if you don't know how well you've done? In fact, how well have you done? Do you know where your strengths and weaknesses are? If you found out where they are what changes might you make, if any?

This is a lot of questions, but they all need to be answered honestly. For instance, if you maintain records on the ratios of those customers who did not buy certain products to customers who did buy, you can establish certain things: are your questioning skills thorough enough and what, if any, training can be applied to improve the questioning skills which will ultimately increase the sales achieved? Are you selling to only a particular type of customer or a specific part of the community? Alternatively, are you in need of additional rapport building skills or the most obvious skill of closing?

There is an old adage which states:

**"If you always do what you've always done,
...you'll always get what you always got!"**

How does this saying relate to you? Are you ready to change? Unless you make some changes nothing will change. If you are ready then you need a plan and a direction.

If you keep records on yourself and your clients, do you refer back to them? Do you contact your previous clients? Again a suitable plan is required to make effective use of this information.

How does all this record-keeping relate to closing? It really relates to establishing a record of your successes and failures, and by analysing this information you should effect a pro-active development plan which will permit you to clearly focus on your strengths and weaknesses and be in a position to know exactly what is required for you to build on the successes thus far achieved and to attain the high standards you wish to aspire to.

Unless you *act* upon the information obtained the records will remain just that... records!!

We feel certain the above will be of benefit to you when you next meet a customer, but please be careful that you do *not* 'talk through the sale'. Sometimes salespeople become so enthusiastic about their product or service, even though I agree enthusiasm is important, they do not stop informing the customer about the many features and associated benefits. The enthusiasm is such that during the early stages the customer has been lifted to a high level of excitement and wants to buy. Unfortunately the inexperienced salesperson does not recognise the evident buying signals displayed by the customer in front of him and continues to talk about the product or service without noticing. Quite often salespeople have been known to 'show off' to a customer their knowledge of the product's features.

Remember we said earlier that too much knowledge is dangerous. The end result leaves the customer frustrated and even bored to the extent they decide to move on and fail to buy anything. The salesperson has effectively lost the sale by 'talking through' the sale, mentally lifting the customer, failing to close, and consequently remain talking right out of the other side, without achieving a sale at all. What a waste of time for all concerned!

So in summary, what we mean by working **S.M.A.R.T.E.R.** is; **S**kills, **M**onitor, **A**ttitude, **R**ealistic, **T**iming, **E**xperience and **R**ecords. Applying these, in addition to knowing how and when to ask for Referrals will greatly increase your chances of success, for remember it Now Really Is YOUR Turn For Success!

Referrals and Repeat Business

Okay, so you've followed the Sales Process all the way through and are now in the happy position of having completed the sale of your product or service – what next? The pressure is off, you have made the sale and do you now just relax? Not yet! Should you just leave as quickly as possible, or ask the customer to? Should you stand and socialise for a further twenty minutes and overstay your welcome? Or is there another alternative, and yet very effective, use of your time at this point?

Obtaining Referrals and Repeat Business is an extraordinarily good and productive use of your time after completing a sale and when used correctly will show a significant increase in the amount of sales and subsequent business you can generate. This section will provide additional guidance on how to further increase your chances of success by regularly securing many productive Referrals and also obtaining Repeat Business.

Referrals

Before we explain this in more detail we should firstly confirm what is meant here when using the term 'referral'. A referral in this context is where an existing customer passes to you the details – name, phone number, etc. – of someone else whom they believe may also be interested in your products or services, either to buy them or to sell them. Thus they are 'referring' you to someone else whom they know. As such these referrals are extremely valuable to the continuing growth and development of your business and should be sourced wherever and whenever possible.

But where do you start to source referrals and why ask for them anyway?

Do you in fact ask for them? If not, why not? How should you ask for them? When is the best time to ask for referrals? What do you do if you do not receive a referral? Again this is a lot of questions but questions which need to be asked; and answered! As with 'closing' the timing is very important when asking for referrals. You will find it particularly difficult to obtain a referral should you have in some way upset the customer. Also, it will be difficult (but not impossible) to ask if you have not been able to success-fully negotiate a satisfactory sale. However, if you have presented yourself, the company and the product or services you have to offer professionally, do you think the customer may refer others to you? And what will be the benefit to you (and your network) if this occurred?

When you first start in this industry one of the recognised hardest parts of the role is getting to meet sufficient numbers of interest-ed people who you can talk to and subsequently demonstrate your products or services to, which hopefully they will buy. If your success is governed by the number of people who fit the above scenario, and it surely must be, then why continue to make life hard for yourself by having to start at the beginning every time when you need to contact potential customers – 'How hard do you want it to be?' Clearly you do not want it to be any harder than it needs to be. If we could show you a way of making the contact with 'interested' people in a fraction of the time and with almost guaranteed success we are sure you would be interested!

Well, listen very carefully because we are going to share with you the concept and benefits of asking for referrals. From our experience of dealing with many different sales industries one thing always remains intact and that is the need for the salespeople to regularly and consistently ask for referrals in order to increase their sales and their income. It will also contribute to the company's turnover or more precisely the profit.

Unfortunately, the term 'referral' has, in some instances, acquired a rather poor name; for some people it almost ranks with the term begging, and for others the word referral just conjures up thoughts of pleading for help. Well, in truth we can understand how you feel, others have felt like that also, but what they've found is that by using some very simple and straightforward approaches they increase the number of referrals they obtain every time!! (Where have you heard this phrase used before?) Essentially, what is required is a positive and determined approach to the subject and for the salesperson to be fully conversant with the correct method of 'asking' for referrals. Having practised the methods regularly they will build both their own confidence and their own competence to successfully complete the task.

You will need to practise the following phrases and it's important the words should 'fit your own mouth' or to put it another way, the phrases should be put into *'your own words'* so that you are comfortable with them and they do not sound false, scripted or in any way insincere. What you will be creating is your very own record of the types of phrases to use in a given situation and this should unquestionably ensure you increase your chances of success when obtaining referrals.

Before we consider the phrases let's just consider one more thing. Remember the example given earlier where we had a customer just agree to buy your product or service – when do you think is the best time to actually ask for the referral? Many people fail to obtain referrals because they undoubtedly ask for it at the wrong time and as we know with much of the Sales Process, timing is everything. Should you ask before you sell anything, after the customer has agreed to buy but before they sign any paperwork or part with any money, or should you ask once the admin. has been completed, the order placed and you are about to leave?

The right time to ask

From our experience the precise timing will vary slightly from industry to industry but without question what is a very successful time to ask for a referral is straight after the customer has agreed to buy and has signed the necessary paperwork (commitment) and or parted with money, either by way of a deposit or as full payment. The reason this time is so successful is because of the following factors:

    i.   the customer likes and trusts you

    ii.   the customer likes the product or service (and possibly the company)

    iii.   the customer has been convinced of its merit and wants it

    iv.   the customer has already agreed to buy and as such feels good…

    v.   …they may feel good but they could also feel guilty – cost, spouse/partner influence

    vi.   the customer will need reassuring they made the right decision

    vii.   the customer may want to tell everyone what they have bought – pride/pleasure

It is incumbent on the salesperson to meet the concerns, if they exist, within v. and vi. above as the customer may need reassuring they made the correct decision when buying and quite often customers have 'second thoughts' about the purchase almost immediately after buying. This is often known as the guilt period – have I made the right decision, what will my spouse/partner say when they know I've spent money on this item or how can I explain this purchase to my friends? Therefore now is a good time to eradicate such concerns by thanking the customer for their purchase, confirming they made the right decision and reassuring them that their friends, family or colleagues will appreciate this purchase for a long time to come.

At this time you are resettling the customer's mind towards the definite belief they made the right decision after all. To confirm this in their mind you can now ask the following selection of questions:

Mr/Ms Customer, let me ask you:

- are you happy with the service I have provided? Or;
- you are happy with the service I have provided, aren't you?
- are you happy with the product or service which you have just purchased? Or;
- you are happy with the product or service which you have just purchased, aren't you?
- do you agree that you have received an excellent product/service?
- do you agree that this product/service is just what you required?
- do you know of anyone else who might be interested in this and the other products?
- do you know of anyone else who may be interested in earning money from promoting these products?
- who do you know who may be interested in purchasing these products?
- who do you know who may be interested in earning money from promoting this range of products or services?

As you can see the initial questions are a soft leader to confirm the customer is satisfied with both the service they have received from you and their desire for the product or service which they have just purchased. A couple are designed to be somewhat leading questions in that you are almost telling the customer 'they are satisfied with the service they have received and the products they have just purchased, aren't they', and as such are a useful variation. Ultimately they strive to obtain 'yes's from the customer and to get them into the frame of mind to continue to say 'yes'. We mentioned the importance of getting the customer to say 'yes' earlier and this is a continuation of the same process. It reconfirms in their mind, subconsciously and consciously, that they made the 'right decision'. Next the questions move onto the subject of who else the customer may know who could benefit from the products or services offered.

Initially, as we discussed much earlier in this book, the customer will know many many people, but what we need to achieve is the customer to focus on a select few – it could be friends, family, work colleagues or neighbours – it does not necessarily matter who they are but that they fit a certain profile – they believe the individuals will have an interest or desire for the product/service – by channelling the customer's thoughts down a few selected paths they are much more likely to recall people's names, phone numbers, etc., so rather than just stick with the 'who' do you know make the question more focused – 'who do you know at work/at your aerobics class/at the golf club/from your family who may be interested in the products or services which I have demonstrated to you?'

This type of question will allow them to focus on selected individuals and is much more successful in obtaining good and ultimately productive referrals.

Another way of approaching the topic of referrals with customers is at the same timing moment (after the sale has been completed and the customer is still on a high) ask them to consider how you first met this customer. Quite possibly you may have been introduced by someone else, a friend, neighbour, colleague, relation or just an acquaintance. Either way there is a possibility you were 'introduced' to the individual. As a result you have established a good working relationship, maybe even a social relationship, and therefore you have established yourself as both honest, sincere and trustworthy. Coincidentally, as you both met through a 'friend of a friend', as it were, there is every likelihood they will know of other people whom you could go and talk to about your products or services, etc., etc...

As a salesperson, it is the expansion of this introduction process which can open many more doors and contacts for you. How? If indeed you were introduced to the customer then there is a strong possibility you were advised of certain factors about the individual even before you finally met them – they were married, single or divorced, their occupation and even where they live are all bits of information which you discovered prior to even talking to them and discussing your products or services. It is this background information which can be so useful when considering the actual products or services which are likely to be most useful and beneficial to them and therefore which you may consider showing to them upon your eventual initial meeting.

Forward planning never does any harm and to quote an often used phrase: 'To be forewarned is to be forearmed'. Essentially this information lets you know some of the circumstances of the individual before you contact them and in the sense it's better to know this detail than not to know it, since it helps you build an image of their potential requirements long before you meet them.

However, beware you do not start jumping to too many conclusions; best wait until you meet the referral before you start placing their order and banking their money!

We should also add that you will need to be discreet about the information you obtain by keeping all the details you collect on each customer confidential. You do not want a previously satisfied and happy customer suddenly discovering that you have been telling everyone else exactly what they had bought or that you had been disclosing details about their personal situation, especially if the product or service they had purchased was of a medical or financial nature. Naturally, if the customer is agreeable to you disclosing the purchases they have made on the basis that it will assist with the development of your business (for it surely will) then that is fine, but best obtain their agreement first. Remember to maintain the 'trust' you worked hard to establish at all times.

In conclusion, on the basis your customer is satisfied with you, your company and your product or service – and they must be relatively happy with these because they have just bought something from you after all – there will always be an opportunity to ask for referrals; all you need to do is ask.

The benefit of timing your request for a referral correctly is that the client will happily provide a referral(s) as a way of expressing their satisfaction with you and your service, which will ultimately increase the potential for future sales.

Therefore, remember the best time to ask for a referral is invariably at the point when the customer has just purchased your product(s) or service(s). This is likely to be when they are at a high point of satisfaction from the service they have received and also they will be filled with the expectation of owning and using the product(s) they have just purchased.

Remember:

'The method of asking for the referral should form part of the natural Sales Process.'

Finally, you should always be asking for referrals – not just to buy the products *but also to become distributors.* However, rule number one is to 'Keep It Simple'.

Don't get involved in complex calculations about how they can become very, very rich. Simply point out to the individual how easily they could afford to pay off the outstanding loan/buy the kid's birthday present/have a holiday, etc., etc. Keep the examples realistic and achievable.

Do *not* tell them they will be millionaires by Christmas!!

Once you have got them interested, at a later date you can go into more detail but not too much detail (as with the product knowledge we discussed earlier); too much detail too quickly may frighten them off – keep it simple. We will look at recruiting in more detail in Chapter Eight. But for now let's consider ways to secure regular Repeat Business…

Repeat Business

On the subject of Repeat Business, a great deal of Repeat Business is derived from the source we have just discussed and that is referrals. Much business is generated through word of mouth, as mentioned earlier – a well-treated and satisfied customer *may* tell two or three friends of how well they were treated by a salesperson/company but a dissatisfied customer *will* tell dozens of people – this statement is never more true when attempting to obtain Repeat Business. How many customers who are dissatisfied with the products, service or lack of attention from the salesperson will continue to buy? *Very few.*

So how do you ensure you secure the maximum potential for Repeat Business from your customers? One way is to offer a 'discount' on the purchase price of the products (if possible) by effectively passing on a portion of the discount which you will secure from the increased orders obtained (see Chapter Two, 'Is That What I Can Earn?', for more details). Alternatively, use this method but apply a discount to products which the customer has not yet tried thereby encouraging them to try other products available from your company. Another way to increase the potential for Repeat Business is to maintain regular personal contact with the customer – they never forget you and recognise that *you* are the person from whom they buy XYZ products. This is all about providing a service to the customer and is something which this book has highlighted and expounded throughout and will almost certainly guarantee success for you on many occasions.

Another opportunity to secure Repeat Business is to contact the customers when *new* products or services are introduced by your company as this allows an ideal medium to generate increased sales and enhanced volume production. Certainly not an opportunity to be missed!

In addition to these occasions to increase your Repeat Business is quite possibly the most obvious of all, that is to promote and sell the products for which the customer will have an unending requirement – items which only last for a short period like 'consumables' where they run out after a month or three months and therefore the customer will have to buy more product or go without.

Now if your product is something which the customer uses regularly like cosmetics, perfumes, personal care, weight-loss, household and automotive products, there will inevitably be a requirement for further orders in the not too distant future as the products run out.

Securing Repeat Business can be as easy or as hard as you want it to be and "How hard do you want it to be?" If you pay attention to your customers and give attention to their requirements like service and assistance, the customer will return time and again for many years to come.

We wonder how many of the referrals you are about to contact will become customers and how many you will retain as customers if you fail to keep in touch with them on a regular basis? It is important to take heed of what we have said here because, from our experience in many different markets and across many different countries, providing good quality service is paramount to the long-term success of your business.

As the great Lee Iococca, who was the President of Chrysler cars in the USA, once said:

"When product and price are inseparable people will buy from the company which provides the BEST SERVICE"

Please take a moment to consider that statement…

It must be realised why people buy and what processes are involved in the purchase. Lee knew that service, and especially *good* service, was paramount to the future success of the company. His philosophy combined with his newly acquired position within the large American car market had ensured all his employees adopted the above approach to *all* present and future customers across the whole country. Quite a task to take on board, but absolutely necessary for the company's survival.

Thus he was to turn the company from the brink of bankruptcy into one of the most successful and top fifty placed companies in the world.

Another quote relating to providing service to customers, which also made the headlines some years ago, and although much longer is no less significant:

"Probably the most important management fundamental that is being ignored today is staying close to the customer to satisfy his needs and anticipate his wants. In too many companies, the customer has become a bloody nuisance whose unpredictable behaviour damages carefully made strategic plans, whose activities mess up computer operations, and who stubbornly insists that purchased products should work."

Lew Young, Editor-in-Chief, *Business Week*

Again the concept for the salesperson (and management) to grasp is that the customer is the key to any business; in fact without them your business would simply not exist. Whether it's Direct Sales or Multi-Level Marketing, the customer is always going to be king!

People buy from people and providing good service can make a big difference. The most successful salespeople in the industry are those who correctly match the needs of their customer with the benefits of the product or service, where the customer does not so much feel they have been 'sold to' but more that they made a conscious and positive decision to 'buy' the product or service!

The quality of service they received along the way from the salesperson will have provided them with confidence in his/her ability and satisfaction in the attention to detail, certainly a salesperson they would have no hesitation in recommending to others – and often they do so.

Now that you are armed with all this new-found wealth of knowledge and understanding, especially relating to ways of becoming even more successful at closing and obtaining referrals, we must caution you to ensure that you constantly work at developing these skills and thereby maintain your objective – to achieve even greater success!

Learning Points From Chapter Five:

1. When closing the sale, I am aware that timing is important in order to successfully complete the sale.

2. I understand S.M.A.R.T.E.R. and consistently follow the process.

3. Do you have records of who your customers are? Do these records include what was ordered, and when they need to be contacted for repeat products?

4. Satisfied customers are the foundation of any successful business. Do you regularly ask for and receive referrals?

5. I have implemented a method to ensure that the members of my network regularly ask for and obtain referrals.

Notes:

_____

_____

_____

_____

Chapter Six

Up And Running

Now that you have started to learn, practise and develop many of the fundamental requirements to ensure success in either industry, you can start on the next step towards even greater success. Firstly we must not forget the skills already learned for these form the foundation for building on; they form part of the basic and rudimentary requirements all successful agents and distributors need to acquire. These individuals will not have attained the success they have achieved without first knowing and implementing many of the skills you are learning here and now.

Whilst we hesitate to refer to this early stage as an 'apprenticeship' for all that name implies, it is none the less a very big learning curve which anyone new to the industries, and some who have been here for a while, discover they have to climb. The good news is that you have made it this far (and you are still reading the book) so something must be working right!

Incidentally, if you are a reader who has been in the industry for some time I hope you have not just flicked straight to this chapter as you will have missed a variety of useful and creative ideas to assist with your business in the preceding chapters. Perhaps you should refer to them now before continuing because we want you to maximise the benefits derived from reading the complete book.

We considered in an earlier chapter one decision you need to make when joining an MLM or Direct Sales Company, and that is whether or not you join on a full-time basis or a part-time basis. Whichever option you chose, it might be an appropriate time to evaluate that decision and consider in more detail each role in turn.

Full-time agents/distributors

What do they do? Essentially, the full-time distributor will recruit and sell the product all day and teach others to do the same.

How is this done? They will have more time available to talk to you and existing people, talk about the product (or service) and talk about the opportunity. What do you talk about? Talk about the testimonials, yours and others, about the product and about the opportunity.

They will hold what is known as an 'Opportunity Meeting' on a regular basis, possibly once a week, where they will provide advisory and informative sessions about the company, the products or services and about the 'opportunity'. This may be how you became aware of the 'opportunity' which exists for you. The aim of such meetings is to obtain new recruits to join their network.

On other occasions they will conduct Product Training sessions to assist with improving the knowledge and potential sales ability of the individuals in their network. These sessions are not designed to make experts and may be conducted by more than one full-time agent or distributor to allow for maximum numbers attending from different groups and also to provide variety in presentation styles. As the term implies, it is a *full-time* role and when used efficiently (more on this in Chapter Eight) will secure an extremely good standard of living and a source of regular (sometimes substantial) income.

Part-time agents/distributors

What does a part-time distributor do? They will recruit and sell the products in the time they have available and will teach others to do the same.

How do they do this? Part-time distributors usually have a limited amount of time available due to other commitments – another job, family, etc. They find excuses to talk to people. They arrange events like a coffee morning and demonstrate the products. In addition, they should take the time to explain the opportunity which exists for the attendees to join the company as a distributor. They will contact people who advertise in local and national papers, as these are excellent lead sources, costing no more than a telephone call, and arrange to talk to them about the business opportunity (often full-time agents/distributors will adopt this particular method as well).

They may arrange a party – make up invitation cards and invite about fifteen to twenty people, even placing small advertisements in newspapers to promote the event. Another method utilised is to use trade shows and exhibitions to recruit and sell the products.

In many respects there are tremendous similarities in the roles of full-time and part-time agents/distributors – essentially they are both promoting the products and the opportunity.

How to increase your market share

It will be beneficial at this point to consider in more detail exactly how you should promote and market your products or services. In either an MLM or Direct Sales company there will be many different ways to market your particular company's products and services and essentially this is known as 'retailing' the product.

It is most likely that your own company will have their ideas about the 'best' methods to adopt. It's quite possible they will offer many tried and tested ways to achieve success when promoting their specific products or services and you should heed their advice. Some of the key ways are briefly described for you below;

1. Buy and use the products or services yourself – obvious but essential.
2. Family and friends – close circles of influence (How many people do you 'know'? Remember that statistics show on average, it's 25,000 people?!).
3. Referrals – use Testimonials (your own or other people's) effectively.
4. Use car stickers/badges/cards – promoting the company and *you*.

5.   Place ads/flyers – suitably worded lineage ad or cleverly designed flyers to promote.
6.   Direct approaches – fit into day-to-day life, talk to people in lifts/queues/buses/trains, etc.
7.   The more people you talk to about what you do the more successful you will become.
8.   Observe the *three rules for success*.

This is quite an active list to work on and in time, and with growing experience, we expect you will discover many other methods (hopefully ethical) of promoting, marketing and ultimately selling your products or services to lots of customers.

Buy and use the products or services yourself

The first method identified above is the most obvious and logical place to start – you start buying and using the products yourself; the likely outcome of this will lead to your *family and friends* also buying the products or services. As explained earlier, you will have a wealth of people you can begin talking to before you ever need to start talking to 'strangers'. And because you now know how to obtain *referrals,* especially from your family and friends, it's quite likely that even a potentially 'new' person you get to talk to will be known, at least in part. You must also look for other sources of customers and recruits because there will always be ample people to meet and a never-ending amount of opportunities to fulfil.

Use car stickers/badges/cards

The use of stickers, badges and business cards (or introduction cards), is becoming more widespread these days as their value as a marketing and promotional tool has been realised by more and more people. It is a great way to alert people to what you do, who you represent or just to arouse their curiosity about what you do.

Many times we have heard of exciting stories unfolding and much business being generated all because the agent or distributor started a conversation with someone based around a particular comment on the badge or sticker they had been wearing.

One distributor we know of obtained over one hundred new recruits in another country, all of which produced exceedingly good business production, just by asking a few questions during an informal discussion in a lift! He simply took the initiative and using a pre-prepared presentation went for it, and what a result! ("How hard do you want it to be?")

As good a story as this is, sadly this will not always happen, but if you do not prepare yourself and try in the first place you will never know of the lost opportunity waiting just around the corner or in the next lift!

Place ads/flyers

Another way of alerting people to what you do comes in the form of advertisements and what is known as 'flyers'. A flyer is a form of leaflet left strategically for the intended customers to find – through their door, on their car windscreen, handed out in the street, etc. – but there is a cost involved in producing such items and if you get the message wrong, very few will buy. It may be advisable to take advice from your own particular company on this method also, because there is likely to be legislation surrounding what you can and what you cannot say about the products or services being promoted.

Overall, this method can produce business for you but it is very time-consuming and can be expensive (printing costs, delivery, etc.); whilst it does get your name/company/products or services in front of people it should be used *in addition* to other methods. We do not suggest you rely solely on this method of promoting yourself.

Direct approach

As seen in the example given above, one of the best methods of obtaining meetings, promoting your products or services, recruiting new members, etc. is to create the opportunity yourself.

When in a lift, or in a queue, on a train or a bus, virtually any time you are close to other people try the 'Direct Approach'. Talk to people, without being too pushy or rude, be sincere and strike up a conversation.

One big advantage of this method is that you can fit it into your day-to-day life, talking to people when it's convenient. Once you have made contact ask genuine questions like: "Where do you live?" They will reply with, 'Anytown'. You go on to say, "That's great. I'm looking for someone who lives in Anytown to help me with my business…" This leads you straight into your brief pre-prepared presentation about precisely 'how' they can help you *and* themselves!

It's usually better and highly recommended for you to arrange another meeting with the individual, rather than discuss too many specifics in a lift or a bus queue!

Another question to try after you have established some rapport and when sourcing new contacts is: "Maybe you could help me with my business… who do you know who has a car?" This allows them to consider various people and supply quite possibly an answer or at least ask a question like, "Why do you want to know?" Here you have the person's interest, and this again allows you to continue with a short pre-prepared presentation, covering the benefits of your products or services and the opportunity which may exist for them. Afterwards, you can arrange a subsequent meeting where you can discuss your proposals in more detail.

If you have not done so already, you should try this method of contacting people and securing their interest. Use the **S.I.G.N.** acronym (we shall discuss this shortly) **S**timulate **I**nterest and **G**enerate **N**eeds – it works!

The more people you talk to…

When I (Richard) started selling in the Direct Sales industry in 1985 I was told a very useful piece of information and something that I shall share with you today. I remember this piece of information as if it were told to me only yesterday… that is how great the impact of it was.

I was at a monthly meeting, my *first* monthly meeting in fact, and I was unsure where to sit. Should I sit at the front, the back, at the side – where? I decided to sit one row back from the front, second seat in from the central isle. I was keen!

A man came and sat beside me shortly before the start of the meeting and we both greeted each other with the usual courtesies. I didn't really know who he was aside from his name and he didn't really know who I was either! We briefly talked and I mentioned that I had only just joined the company. The meeting started and eventually he was introduced by the person leading the meeting as the company's *top achiever.*

He had personally earned, in the last year alone, over £240,000 and his 'business' was currently worth in excess of £1 million. He was *good!!!*

He began talking and I thought "With credentials like these, this is a guy I should listen to..." He explained his 'story' (with 'drama') and how he got started in the business. I remembered a great deal of what he said and took copious notes (as you can imagine) but the one thing he said that had a lasting impression on me was:

"When you start in this business it is imperative
that you tell everyone you meet what it is that you do...
the more you tell, the more you will sell!"

Curiously, this is as true today as it was in his and my time. You need to tell everyone you meet – not just friends and family – but *everyone* you meet. People at work, on the bus, at your clubs (social or sports) – everyone. *"The more you tell, the more you will sell."* And don't restrict it to just weekdays, talk to people about what you do in the evenings, at weekends, on holiday – everyone!

At the fear of becoming a bore you might be inclined to place certain restrictions on how often you raise the subject whilst at home, for if it continues uncontrolled and unabated, your spouse/partner may want to divorce you, the kids will leave home and your friends might just stop calling for a while.

But, unequivocally, the more people you tell about what you are doing the more committed you will become to it. It is a psychological truism that every time you tell someone what you do you will become a little more confident, a little more committed and a little more competent each time.

Eventually, when you have told lots and lots of people your sales will begin to increase. Your own self-confidence and self-belief will grow and grow and as you begin to see the results of your efforts translate into new friendships, new distributors and lots of new money then you will want to tell everyone something else too – how it was that *you* became so successful!

Three rules for success!

Unquestionably, the more people you talk to the greater your success will become. Every major achiever in the sales industry is so because they kept talking to people. In MLM and Direct Sales especially, the Three Rules for Success apply:

SEE THE PEOPLE   SEE THE PEOPLE SEE THE PEOPLE

The people you talk to could buy the product, or know someone who will. They could join you as an agent or distributor, or know of someone who will. And they could contribute significantly towards the success you want to achieve. All this from just talking to people! ("How hard can it be?" – "How hard do you want it to be?")

We mentioned using the **S.I.G.N.** acronym earlier. Here's how it works. Whilst you are talking to people, whether it's in a product (or service) sale situation or during a conversation intending to recruit, you need to ensure you get the **S.I.G.N.** –

S	**STIMULATE**
I	**INTEREST &**
G	**GENERATE**
N	**NEEDS**

In a product sale scenario you will need to refer to the Stepping Stones to Success covered in an earlier chapter (Four), where asking suitable and relevant questions are essential for a sale to result.

In a recruiting meeting again you need to ask questions in order to 'Stimulate their Interest and Generate their Needs'; in each case you will need to convey exciting and believable claims about the product(s) or about the potential which exists. We strongly recommend you do not mislead the individual for, as also mentioned earlier, this could lead to severe consequences.

For more specific information about recruiting we suggest you refer to Chapter Eight entitled 'How Many People?'

In a product sale you could ask the potential customer key questions like;

- ❖ "Are you serious about losing weight?"
- ❖ "How much weight would you like to lose?"
- ❖ "What have you tried before?"
- ❖ "How soon do you need to lose the weight?"
- ❖ "Do you have a special reason for wanting to lose weight?"

A variation on these questions can be asked of someone who wants skin-care or cosmetic products, etc.

Can you see how this type of questioning stimulates interest?

Once you have successfully achieved this skill in questioning the customer will more likely succumb to your 'focused' presentation skills and these same questioning skills can be applied to recruiting. Some distributors find tremendous success can be achieved by utilising a 'presentation folder' which will include say, pictures of the before and after of the weight loss or show the improved skin quality, etc.

A suitable picture really can speak a thousand words and becomes a 'silent salesman'. Again Testimonials – examples of success – together with the associated 'story' or more precisely the *drama* will increase the success achievable. The *drama* is *very* important and its value should not be underestimated – make it relevant, make it interesting and make it 'real'!

Your Drama should convey to the customer, or recruit, the 'real' story behind what can be achieved. As a child it's quite likely that you would enjoy telling stories of some sort, or at least having them read to you. By creating some Drama in your story about what the benefits are of the products, services or the opportunity, you will ensure the customer or recruit will retain their interest and identify with the needs and wants you have successfully conveyed can be satisfied.

Within your Presentation Folder the products or services only need to be briefly mentioned in bullet point style to ensure the point gets across. All of this information is extremely valuable for you when building and developing your business. But in all cases it is important you have a plan of action…

Your action plan

You may recall, in an earlier chapter we mentioned the value in having an objective and more particularly a 'direction' with your business; there is an often quoted phrase used and we make no apology for repeating it here;

"Nobody plans to fail, but most people do fail to plan"

Therefore, in order to increase the chances of your success even further we suggest you take heed of the following:

- Allow sufficient time for success

- Attend as many appropriate meetings as possible

- Ensure you initially complete a list of at least one hundred names to contact and regularly update it

- Keep learning about network marketing

- Learn about the products or services

- Commit yourself to talk to a certain number of people every day

- Commit yourself to sell products at every opportune moment

- Commit yourself to sponsor a certain number of people every week

- Commit yourself to show company literature to a certain number of people every week

- Commit yourself now – write out the list and follow it through

By following these guidelines, as many other successful agents and distributors will have done before you, and many others will now strive to achieve, you will be *planning for your own success!!*

If that is what you want to achieve you had better start completing your list straight away. Although, just in case you need even more assistance with your plan for success, you might want to finish this chapter first!

Weekly plan sheet

You need to create a weekly plan sheet, and follow it. Keep your diary with you at all times, and whether you use a diary, notepad or electronic diary, it does not really matter, just ensure that whichever method you use, *you make use of it.*

It should always be with you, because as and when various people want your time – customers, distributors, family – you will be able to inform them immediately when you are available, and by liaising with their respective diary you can confirm the date and time there and then. This will virtually eliminate wasted calls, wasted journeys and wasted time!!

In addition, by carrying the diary with you it will enable you to operate your business much more professionally and also more efficiently. You will find that by making time to schedule in specific business, social and family events accordingly, you will never miss such events again!

Let's discover how well you think you are currently doing with managing your time. Try completing the exercise opposite to establish how well *you* believe you are currently managing both your time and your various activities. To be effective, this questionnaire needs to be completed as honestly as possible! Mark a cross in the applicable section: Never, Rarely, Mostly or Always.

Also it will be useful if you complete the section marked 'Suggestions for Improvement' to aid with identifying the specific areas where you feel you require additional assistance. After completing this section as fully as possible you may choose to discuss the areas identified with your upline or sponsor, in order to obtain assistance with this area of your personal development. In addition, you may also obtain benefit from reading the remainder of this book, as the subject of Time Management arises more than once in the process of leading you towards the success you desire.

SELF-ANALYSIS QUESTIONNAIRE

Name: _____

Date: _____

Time Management – General	NEVER	RARELY	MOSTLY	ALWAYS
1. Do I currently use a diary?				
2. Do I plan each day *before* it happens?				
3. Do I prioritise the events and activities?				
4. Do I always attend the diarised events?				
5. Do I regularly review my planning schedule?				
6. Do I make the 'best' use of my time?				
7. Do I know where my time is wasted?				
8. Do I compile a daily 'to do' list?				
9. Do I delegate any suitable tasks?				
10. Do I care what happens?				
Time Management – Personal & Family	NEVER	RARELY	MOSTLY	ALWAYS
1. Do I schedule 'personal' time into my diary?				
2. Do I meet the events scheduled?				
3. Do I schedule 'family' time into my diary?				
4. Do I meet the events scheduled?				
5. Do I control the stress trying to meet these deadlines?				
6. Do I consider this time is time well spent?				
7. Do I make the 'best' use of my personal and family time?				

Time Management – Business	NEVER	RARELY	MOSTLY	ALWAYS
1. Do I set aside time to plan my business direction?				
2. Do I effectively utilise the resources available?				
3. Do I focus on the key elements necessary to increase my business?				
4. Do I devote sufficient time to urgent and important things?				
5. Do I know how to deal with time wasters?				
6. Do I always maintain a positive attitude?				
7. Do I look for new ways to improve sales volume?				
8. Do I quickly familiarise myself with new products or services?				
9. Do I communicate effectively?				
10. Do I communicate regularly with my downline and upline?				

Suggestions for improvement: _____

_____

_____

_____

How did you get on with the questionnaire? Ideally you will have entered most of your crosses in the 'Always' box. But in the likely event this may not have happened, we suggest you read on to discover how to improve your management of time and therefore, increase your chances of success!

Remember the earlier statement:

**If you don't know where you're going,
how are you going to know when you get there?**

This also comes into the planning and Time Management aspects of your business. You need to know where you are going, who you are seeing and when, and also perhaps, why? When you are planning your diary, you need to cover three sections, your Family Time, your Personal Time (which can include your spiritual time) and your Business Time.

The first thing to mark out of your diary is your family time, for they may see less of you once you become very busy and it's important to schedule in time for them. Next it's your personal time, the time you need for yourself, to study, socialise or just relax! And then you must build in some time for developing your business – work time. Hopefully there will be some time left in your diary for this?

There is no such thing as a 'lack of time' as we all have adequate time to do everything we really want to do. That's quite a statement, but it's based around the precept that you are making sure you carefully 'plan' the time you have available each day, and this is the key.

We all have just 7 days in a week, or the equivalent of 168 hours or 10,080 minutes, no matter which country you live in or which country you come from – how do you spend yours? If you feel, like many people, that you are always 'too busy' then you will enjoy what we shall be sharing with you in the remainder of this chapter.

Effective use of your time is like driving a car – it's a skill that can be acquired and improved upon no matter how good you currently think you are, and hopefully by the end of this chapter you will possess a greater understanding of the control and satisfaction you can take in your life by discovering, utilising and improving the management of your time.

We are not attempting to turn you into a 'guru' or 'time lord' on the subject, just provide you with some simple and yet fundamental facts about effective use of your time.

Did you have an entire day free from your busy schedule to set aside to read this book? Did you have to juggle appointments/meetings/training sessions? We would suspect that you had to do some planning to free up sufficient time to be able to read this book and for those of you who have no idea about time management, or feel that you could improve your time management, you have just taken the first step.

In fact you have allowed yourself the luxury of investing in this book and making time away from the hustle and bustle of your busy lives, to give yourself the start to taking better control of your business and of your time, and thereby become even more effective and productive.

Planning (direction!)

In order to help you appreciate the importance of effective planning and the importance of creating a 'direction' or route map for both you and your business to follow, please take a few moments to consider this scenario:

> If we were to take you from where you are seated, blindfold you and put you in a car and drive for an 'assumed' time of five hours (real time will not be known – you can't see your watch!), then make you walk for a further two (assumed) hours across unknown terrain, and finally remove your blindfold and leave you without a compass, map or any appreciable method of knowing where you are – how would you find your way back to where you had started? Always assuming you would want to find your way back there... !!

From your new location, what are the things you would need to clearly establish *first!?*

Aside from the more obvious survival factors – accessibility to water, food and shelter and possibly at some stage the need for money – you should be considering a short list which will include quite simply, the following:

*   Where am I now?
*   Where do I need to be?
*   What is the best method of getting me there?

This principle has several names, but the most common is 'The Broad Concept'. It can apply in a very wide range of diverse topics. In the above example you need to establish 'where you are now' before you know in which direction to set off.

This could be tricky to establish but with some simple logic – location of the sun, noting any landmarks and having taken mental notes whilst undertaking the journey – you will be able to create a 'guestimate' as to where you are located. Although it is only a *'guestimate'* and nothing more, it is something to build on and to add to as you travel and discover more about your location.

In the early stages of your journey it is quite likely that you will feel somewhat stressed by the situation, the unfamiliar surroundings, and the lack of anything or anyone you can relate to. You may become filled with the desire to be 'home', or at least to feel safe and secure!

Quite soon you may uncover a clue as to your approximate location – north, south, east or west from your starting point – and this in turn will assist you in making some general fine tuning to the route you need to take in order to arrive back at the starting point.

Occasionally you will go down a path which will turn into a dead end (*cul de sac*) or you may discover it's actually taking you completely the wrong way. Inevitably, some more adjustments, or fine tuning, will be necessary *en route*.

Once you start to recognise more familiar landmarks or streets and roads the journey will be less stressful, more enjoyable (accomplishment) and to an extent, satisfying (you were *not* beaten!) Once you are in these familiar surroundings it is likely that you will more precisely be able to assess the time taken before you arrive at your destination.

Finally, you will arrive back at your starting point, with a great deal of self-satisfaction (and rightly so) from your achievement. So what has all this got to do with planning and managing your time?

Well, a few pages ago we asked you to complete a 'Self-Analysis Questionnaire' indicating how you currently manage your time – Where are you now? – and this provides you with much of the information you probably already knew but did not have to hand in quite this format.

Ideally you should now complete a second form indicating how you wanted to be, or thought you should be, managing your time – Where do you want to be? – and this will inevitably show some differences in your desired management of time compared to your actual management of time.

Finally, we must consider some ways and methods of making more effective use of the time you have available – What is the best method of getting you there? – and careful and effective *planning* is the key to all of this.

So this 'Broad Concept' will work in virtually any situation and with virtually any combination of circumstances/people/constraints. It also helps with your personal and team motivation as it assists with the development of a 'goal' and provides the opportunity to design or create a 'direction' for either you, your team or your organisation to take.

As you will appreciate;

"It is far easier to hit the target if you can see it!"

and

**"If you know where you are going
you are much more likely to get there!"**

We are now moving into another area which is covered in much greater detail on a selection of our courses, but for the benefit of this book, the principle still very much applies here.

Setting time aside to *plan* is important and the best time is either at the start or end of the day – your mind may be more alert first thing in the morning and allow you the freedom, without the worries and hassles that the day will bring, to devote to careful and constructive time for planning.

Alternatively, you may be the type of person who is better suited to completing the task of planning at the end of the day, for the day's events are still fresh in your mind and you can't leave work until you've listed down all of the requirements for tomorrow.

Either way will work, in fact some people find a combination of both to be the most effective, whereby you review how successful (or not) you have been at the end of the day in accomplishing the tasks on your 'to do' list and this in turn helps to contribute towards your plans/list for tomorrow. In any event, setting aside time for proper planning should be time well spent.

There are certain people who avidly believe in 'Biorhythms' and that by studying these charts you can best decide at what time of the day/week/month you should complete certain tasks. We don't know about all that; all we know is the time of day when we can work at our best and the time of day when we might be er…, 'less effective'. How about you, do you know what part of the day you are the most effective?

If not we suggest you consider this matter carefully as you may find that you have been preparing or completing certain tasks during a period when you are not at your most alert and decisive or creative/effective – and as a result the finished task is not up to the required standard, either yours or for whom the task was completed.

Incidentally, we are not suggesting here that you should all complete the tasks required during the fifteen minutes of the morning when you feel most alert – after an intake of coffee – or that you should be only working from home, and in the evening at that! No, this subject is quite important in the general scheme of things because it's assessing the time of day/week when you are likely to be at your most productive, constructive and effective.

Remember we asked you about your personal time and your family time? You need to find time for them, as they are probably part of the reason why you work so hard. You want to share the rewards of your hard work with them. Make sure you put some time aside for them. (Blank out several times in the week) Try and ensure you set aside some time at the end of each day to evaluate what was achieved during the day and to set objectives ('to do' list) for tomorrow. This can be particularly helpful if you are slightly forgetful – write it down now whilst it's still fresh in your mind!

Your 'to do' list should be as detailed and accurate as possible. List all the things which need to be completed, not necessarily by the next day, but over a period of time. Primarily document all the tasks associated with your business, both the development of customers and new recruits, and not forgetting your own personal development. Where possible try and separate the personal and family issues into another list. In this example we are focusing on the business aspects of your time management.

A useful tip when planning your time is when you are offering appointment times, remember to offer alternatives. People will accept an alternative. If you only give one time people may say no, and if you leave it to the potential customer or recruit to set the time, it will never happen. You must remember to continually do the basics, talk to people, use the products and distribute company literature. The more you do, the more that will come back to you.

You have been given an introduction into Time Management, and how you can start to use the time you have available to your advantage.

Periodically throughout the book, it is touched on again to remind and assist you. Start to put into action the points we have covered here, and by effectively deciding to actually do something about them it will be seen as a positive step forward, and could also be seen as an effective use of your time. Over a period of time you will inevitably discover improvements to your business, your personal and family life.

We all have to make choices in our life; some are naturally a great deal easier to make than others, and occasionally there will be choices which you have to make where the constraints on you to make a 'free' choice are limited by impossible situations.

But much of the time you will be free to make the choice – how and where you spend your time for instance – you are kidding yourself if you believe outside factors always control your life (occasionally they will) but it could be you that are not making the best of the opportunity which presents itself. When you do have the choice, take control!

One final thought…

…and we've saved the best till last! When confronted with an array of different tasks or if you are in a situation where you are unsure of exactly what you should be doing next, it *will* be helpful if you compile the following statement and place it in a prominent position near/on your desk (or forehead!) to assist;

"WHAT'S THE BEST USE OF MY TIME, RIGHT NOW!?"

Think about this statement… What is the *best* use of *your* time, *right now!?*

If the best use of your time is to read the newspaper, prepare for a meeting, complete the sales forecast or ring your customers to obtain more orders, then that's fine. However, if you are very honest with yourself and decide that quite possibly what you are currently doing is *not* in fact the *best* use of your time then think again… What is the *best* use of *your* time, *right now!?*

It may be the 'best' use of your time is to delegate some tasks to others.

If you start delegating, first you need to check to ensure the person you are delegating the task to is capable of completing it to your standard. If so, then delegate. If not, then think again.

Once you have decided where the best use of your time is, make the change and redirect your use of the time available to ensure you are using your time to the best effect.

With regular practice and constant use this statement will change the way you work, rest and play (sounds like an advert for chocolate!). It's a statement that will constantly make you think about the use of your time and more importantly, it should ensure you are making the *best* use of *your* time…!

So what is the *best* use of your time *right now?*

Hopefully, finishing this book, or at least this chapter!

This time and planning section is not intended to make you ultra efficient with your time and planning, but we hope it will improve your use of time and subsequently provide you with an insight into the kind of 'management' areas you need to be aware of, familiar with and be prepared to regularly practise. In this way it will assist you in your development and ensure you continue on the way to success!

Finally, in this chapter, a great deal of what we have discussed so far will require *confidence* – both in your own ability, in the quality of the company's products or services, and in the benefits the customer will derive from using them.

You should be able to have the utmost *confidence* in *all* of these elements and especially in your own ability, and later within this book we shall explore this avenue in more detail. Meanwhile, let's move on to consider another method of marketing, promoting and selling products, and all by having great fun during a party, at the same time!

Learning Points From Chapter Six:

1. I know which members of my network are full-time and part-time, and I constantly endeavour to help them with their business.

2. I know how to promote and market my business, and I talk to people daily about the opportunity and products.

3. I constantly follow S.I.G.N. and ensure my network also follow the guidelines.

4. I have an action plan that I follow, and so do the members of my network.

5. I have completed the self-analysis questionnaire and I am working on the areas that I need improving.

6. I manage my time as efficiently as I can, giving time to my family, myself and my business.

Notes:

_____

_____

_____

Chapter Seven

Have A Party!

The concept

One of the areas of direct selling that is universal is Party Plan. Some countries call it Home Parties or Home Demonstrations. Whatever the name, it is essentially still the same – Party Plan.

Party Plan is a very successful area of Direct Sales. A group of people, usually women, meet in someone's home (the hostess) and an agent demonstrates a range of products that should be of interest to, and purchased by, the group. For this, the agent receives a commission, usually based on the value of purchases made by the attendees, and the hostess generally receives a gift or a discount towards her own purchases.

This unique system has been around for almost as long as Multi-Level Marketing. However, there are some differences that we will highlight in this chapter and to be successful as a 'Party Planner' there are many areas which you need to take into account.

The main difference from MLM is that generally with Party Plan there is no incentive for the agent to recruit other new recruits. She will not earn any commissions from their sales, as she would if she were in MLM. Sometimes, the Party Plan companies will run a recruiting campaign and then the agent may receive a reward in the form of discounts, gifts or vouchers.

The concept behind Party Plan is that the agent, who works part-time, will use her circle of influence (her close friends and family) and encourage them to hold a 'party' in their home with their friends, so that the agent can demonstrate the products they are selling.

The system is very successful, and there are numerous companies that promote this method of selling. There are also a number of successful MLM companies which do not operate this method, but the agents prefer to promote their products via 'home parties'. This is where a group of people interested in the products gather together, rather than the conventional one on one presentation.

By having a group of people together at the same time, the agent has a greater ability to generate higher sales. The agent has made better use of her time, by introducing her products to many people at the same time. If the hostess has been coached properly, and we will discuss this later, all of those people in her home are there to buy and several will also have the agent come to their home, and demonstrate the products to their friends.

How does the agent coach her hostess? And when does she start? Read on, and discover how to ensure that if you are looking at Party Plan, you are able to make the most of the hostesses you encounter. The guideline will help you to train your hostess to help you achieve higher earnings.

Where do I start?

The first thing you need to do, is find a hostess with plenty of friends! These friends will have friends, who have friends... sounds similar to the structure of an MLM programme?

The hostess first of all needs to choose the products that she would like to buy. From there, if the discount system is in place, she needs to know how much her friends have to buy in order for her to obtain the maximum discount on her purchases. Also, she could find herself with 'extras' in the form of small gifts for the number of friends who book a party with the agent. These 'gifts' are usually selected from within the range of products being sold by the agent.

It is up to you as the agent to help the hostess decide which products she really wants, and which products she would like. The difference here is what level of buying her guests will be required to spend, in order for her to obtain a favourable discount on purchases.

So, the people invited to the party are coming to do one thing – buy products. If they book a party, that is a bonus for the hostess.

In order for your business to be successful, you need to have plenty of 'bookings'. Bookings are the key to the business. The more you have, with plenty of guests, the better your earnings potential.

You need 100% positive attitude when you start – have confidence in yourself, the products, and your ability to train the hostess to invite the guests.

There are many ways to encourage the hostess before the party.

Booking a party

Booking parties is the key to your business. The more you book, the busier you will be. Who are your best booking prospects at a party?

–   The one who buys the most – she obviously loves the product and will want to share it!

–   The most enthusiastic guest – she will have many friends.

–   The best friend of the hostess – she will be delighted to help her friend get more gifts.

–   Relatives of the hostess.

–   The person you seem to relate to best. She'll have a party because she likes you.

–   The busiest person – busy people are organised and have great parties.

Remember...

Bookings begin with you – check your image and attitude. Believe in your product, your desire to share it, and relate this belief and enthusiasm to others. Do you feel there are people too good for your products? If so, you need more product knowledge. You need to develop a proper appreciation for the quality of the products.

Three is the magic number. If you hold three parties a week, you will have more bookings, and be on the way to the income you wanted. The easiest place to book a party is at a party! Act like someone who knows something about this business. Believe in yourself. If you believe you are the best, you will become what you believe.

Booking is simply *asking...* don't be afraid to ask. If a woman indicates she probably would not like to be a hostess, don't just forget it, but ask her why not. If there is an objection, remember — "I understand how you feel, others have felt that way too, but they have found that when they had booked a party, it was very enjoyable/rewarding."

Create a desire in each person to say *yes* to having a party. You are not booking to sell, you are booking to show the products. It will cost the hostess and her friends nothing. Forget about money and sales, they will come automatically. People do not like to be sold to, they like to buy. There is a *big* difference!

Don't worry about getting a *no* answer. Do not take *no* personally. If someone turns you down they are not rejecting you, but the idea of having a party at the present time. They may well change their mind at some stage in the future. Just think about the positive responses you have received and will receive.

Be careful never to criticise another product. If you are asked your opinion about another product, you might say, "I don't know about that, all I know is that ABC products (your company's) are superb quality and good value for money". This approach will help people form a good opinion of you and your company.

Some hints about asking for bookings

Be enthusiastic – prospective hostesses should be able to tell that you love your product, you love to conduct parties, and that you are excited. If you act enthusiastically, you become enthusiastic.

Be confident – you have an excellent product. You love the products or you would not have joined the company. Be confident in yourself... you know more about the products than anyone at the party. Act confidently, continue to learn about your products and you will gain greater competence which will radiate more confidence.

Be persistent – don't take *no* for an answer... go to the next person. You have something to offer your future hostesses. You have a fine product and an opportunity for her to obtain free merchandise. She has *you... and your service.*

Let guests know that you really prefer that parties be kept as simple as possible. You could say, "Those of you who are contemplating booking a party – you will be glad to know that we encourage our hostess to keep the preparation and refreshments simple so that the hostess can also enjoy the party".

It is simple to book future parties from a party. Remember, that the company has a variety of irresistible incentives to offer the hostess.

There is also the possibility that booking gifts can be given to the hostess and prospective hostesses on the night the bookings are taken.

Check with your particular company first to ensure this offer applies, and if it doesn't, why not suggest it's introduced in the future. It can be a very cost-effective way of securing new contacts and extra business.

Before the party:

Leave several catalogues and order forms with the hostess along with a supply of invitations about two weeks before the predetermined day for the party. Tell the hostess to overbook, as some people will be unable to attend. Instruct the hostess to personally deliver the invitations, and explain to the guests that they will pay on the day of the party for the goods they ordered (if applicable) and that she would appreciate their attendance.

Several things will happen – the hostess will know what she wants, and people she invites to the party who cannot come can place an order. There could also be the possibility for someone to want to book a party for themselves as they would not be able to attend the party.

While you are at the hostess's home, check the area that you are going to have available for the party – you need to know beforehand how to set up the display with the space available. You do not want any surprises on the day! Remember the Sales Process stage, number one, 'Preparation'. Prepare yourself and the room/venue.

Also, at this time be enthusiastic with the hostess – she may need her confidence boosting – if this is your first party, you need the support, but remember, this may the first party for the hostess, and you want it to get off to a good start – you will need her again for future parties.

The invitations that are left for the hostess should be given out to her friends, and the invitations need to say where, when and why the party is taking place.

Before the party, the hostess needs to be instructed to contact the people she invited, and confirm that they will attend. This will ensure that people turn up, and that they understand that it is a 'fun' time. Most important – do not bring the kids! We all love having the kids around but not during your party, for they are likely to either disrupt it or distract the guests.

In addition, the same can be said for having pets around during the party. This does not generally produce a very conducive atmosphere for the guests to buy the products and also, the hostess may be put off with the distractions and disturbances and become somewhat distressed, ultimately not booking another party in the future.

On the day of the party:

Make sure that there is an area set aside that will be used for the agent to display the products. Sometimes the agent will have a small table she will bring along, and if this is the case, she will tell the hostess. The agent generally has a cover that she brings as part of her product display.

Make sure that there will be enough seats for the people invited, and that they will be able to see each other comfortably, and more importantly see the products.

When the hostess is preparing for the party, make sure the rest of the family are out of sight; and this includes the pets! You do not want any unnecessary distractions. The focus of the guests should be the products!

The food for the party needs to be kept as simple as possible – tea, coffee, soft drinks and biscuits, and served *after* the agent has shown the products. It is impossible to handle products, eat a biscuit and drink a cup of tea!

Before you leave home:

There are a number of things that you should always have pre-packed, and which will form the foundation for your 'kit' :

- your full product display kit clean, complete and working
- any display aids you want to use – cloth, empty boxes for height, a mirror
- a container with change in it – some people may pay cash!

- your diary and extra pens
- an envelope or folder for the completed orders
- plenty of order forms and invitations, including spare pens

In addition, always ensure you have with you the directions on how to get to the hostess's house, if not already known.

Remember, put your phone number, name and address on all stationery you put out.

Shut the door on housework, children, husband and have a cup of tea or soft drink and gather your thoughts. You have to be confident when you are at the home of the hostess.

Make sure you arrive early, but not too early to fluster the hostess. You must remember that she may be doing last-minute housework or getting ready. Plan for about fifteen to twenty minutes before the party is due to start.

Immediately before the party:

The agent does what is called 'kitchen coaching' with the hostess. What is this? This is merely prompting the hostess to tell the agent who is coming, and a bit of background information about each individual. Such as: what products they like, are they looking for additional income and who else do they know. The agent needs to know which of the guests are the most outgoing, and these people would be the most likely to keep the liveliness of the party going, thus preventing any 'quiet time' from happening. Because of their outgoing personality it is quite likely these guests could also be ideal future hostesses and invite their own circle of friends.

The party:

The hostess will have the agent arrive a short while before the party, to set up and prepare for the guests.

As the guests arrive, the hostess will introduce the guests to the agent, and within a short period of time, other guests will arrive. It is important to start the party at the designated time, and that the party ends at the time set out on the invitations.

It is important to appear friendly and approachable at all times. The guests will be looking at you as the person who will explain the products and how they work, and they will look at you as a person they may invite into their homes to have you do a party for them.

Stand, sit or kneel amongst the guests and try and create an easy and relaxed atmosphere where the guests feel at ease with you and feel free to handle the products you have brought.

As a way to break the ice with the guests, it is advisable that the agent has a number of short, fun games that she can use to get everyone laughing and relaxed with each other, and the agent! Some games that are often used are: coming up with words from the spelling of the company name the agent represents, words that relate to the products on display, or sometimes a pass-the-parcel type of game with a small gift for the winners.

When you are taking the orders from the guests, if someone says that they are unable to purchase what they want, and the reason is lack of money, this person could be an ideal hostess for you for a future party! Quietly talk to her, explain how she could get the products she wants, and then, after everyone has placed their order, announce that this person will be holding a party in several weeks.

By announcing at the party there will be another, several guests will agree to attend, thus building the confidence of the prospective hostess with people who have said yes.

When the party is over, the agent will pack up and leave promptly, thus leaving the hostess and the guests to enjoy themselves.

The agent's role:

The agent's responsibility to the hostess is to arrive early, prepared with products, samples, brochures and knowledge of the products she is selling. After the party, she has the responsibility to ensure that the products are delivered promptly. Most agents will send the hostess a thank-you note for inviting her to their home.

At the beginning of the party, the agent should introduce herself, the company and the products, and thank the hostess for having the party, and everyone for coming along. She should at all times be warm and friendly. Remember, if people like you, they are more likely to buy your products and book a party with you!

At the end of the party, the agent will ask if anyone would like to place an order, and then take the guests one by one to another part of the room, but preferably into another room, and take their orders, and arrange for payments. The reason that you take the guests to one side is to avoid any embarrassment for someone who may not be in a position to buy as much as everyone else, or maybe because of the product wants to speak quietly to the agent before they place their order.

At the end, it is entirely up to the agent and the hostess whether or not the agent tells the guests how much she earned, or how much the hostess earned. Depending upon the company, this is the recruiting time when the agent invites prospective recruits to talk to her about the earning potential of the company. Anyone who is interested, she will take their details and arrange to contact them shortly after the party, ideally within a few days.

After the party:

Some companies will arrange for the products to be sent direct to the customers, the hostess or to the agent. Whatever shipping arrangements are made, the agent needs to clarify for the hostess so that she is aware of what needs to be done. If funds are to be collected, as sometimes happens, an envelope needs to be left with everyone's name written on the outside, along with what amount needs to be paid prior to delivery of the products.

If you are with a company that sends the products to you for distribution to the hostess, this is a wonderful opportunity to place small labels on the products (when appropriate) that are simply marked, 'To re-order contact... phone... ' It is very important for customers to be able to contact you for repeat orders, or to book a party at a future date. It is very easy for people to misplace or throw out the order form or catalogue you have left with them, but if you are able to place a small label on the product, it will be easier for you!

With some products it will not be possible to place labels, so in these instances you will have to hope that a small 'Thank you for your order, if you need any help or want to place further orders please contact... ' card that is attached to the order, or placed in a bag, is sufficient.

Unlike the thank-you note to the hostess after the party, a small thank you for the order note is not commonly used, and yet this is a small, inexpensive way of having the customer or hostess remember you. Some people have a real attitude problem with commission sales. They think that all they need to do is show the products, collect the money and deliver the goods. How wrong can they be!

As we learned earlier in Chapter Five ('Now Is The Time...') good customer service is critical to building a long-term and successful business.

The after-sales service is a key part of ongoing success and a sure way of obtaining repeat and referral business. The small note is a way of showing your customers that you appreciate their order.

If the products are delivered several weeks after the party, and this is very common, a small note reminds the customer just how much they maybe enjoyed themselves at the party.

In addition, it may encourage them to book their own party to hold in their own home and with their own friends. What a potential for you!

It is polite to send the hostess a thank-you note, for the time and effort that was taken to arrange the party. This maintains a good relationship with the hostess and keeps the agent's name in the forefront of their mind should there be any enquiries for the products after the party or any subsequent enquiries for people to hold their own party in the future.

A phone call after the party to the hostess to verify that all is in order is advisable, and at a predetermined time, contact the hostess again for another party.

Giving a party in your own home:

What do you do if you are about to start in the Party Plan business, and you don't have a hostess?

Simple, have your own party!

The principle is the same, except that your guests are prospective hostesses, and you want them to book parties with you. Don't worry about the possibility of a lack of sales. Sales will come from all the future parties booked.

Remember to invite people who you work with, live near, are parents of your children's friends, or even invite some relatives.

Explain that you are just starting out, and need some help in getting started, and that you have chosen those present to help you get started. People are always willing to help.

Personally deliver the invitations, and make sure that the guest is aware that they are helping you with your new business. Call the day before the party to confirm that they will attend. If you make contact with the guests the day before the party, it will help to remind them that they in fact did agree to come, and rather than 'forget' to attend, you will remind them of their commitment.

Who could you invite? You want people who know lots of people, people in clubs, people who work in large offices/factories, people who need to earn a bit of extra cash.

The list of who you can invite is endless, and if you find that you have a large number of people that you can invite, rather than one large party, have several small parties, and mix the people that you invite to each. Make sure that there are people at each party that do not know each other.

By working with several small groups, it will help boost your confidence, and by the time you do your second or third party, any jitters will be gone.

This idea is also great for the hostesses who have a large circle of friends. You may be able to hold two parties with them, and this may be a way to ensure that the majority of the guests do arrive.

How do you ensure the majority will arrive? Quite simple; when the invitation is made, offer them the 'alternate close' which is, "Would you be able to attend Wednesday morning or Thursday afternoon's party?" People will take the option, rather than say no.

This is also a good close to remember when you are booking with your prospective hostesses. Offer them the alternative time when you are booking them into your diary.

Charity parties

Charity parties are a wonderful way of helping to raise funds locally in the community, and they do give you and your products a great deal of exposure. This needs to be handled correctly but first let us answer the most obvious question:

How do they work?

The company that you are with may decide to 'sponsor' a charity for a period of time, and there is then company material available that states a percentage of the sales over a period of time will be donated to a local charity. When this occurs, it is very unlikely that the company will ask the agent to forfeit a portion of their commission. At the end of the period, the company are the ones in the limelight for having contributed to the fund-raising.

However, you as an agent may decide to promote a local charity on your own. You could ask the company for support, but as each company is different, the response could vary from full support to no support. If you do decide to promote a local charity, it will be excellent exposure for you, and could be a way of booking future parties for you. Be aware, however, that you could be asked to do parties to promote another charity. It is up to you how many you will promote.

How do you promote the charity on your own?

The most common way is to set aside a percentage of your commission and pay it to the charity. You may decide that over a period of time a percentage of your commission from all parties will go to a local charity, and you name the charity. When you distribute your invitations, mark clearly on the invite that a percentage of the proceeds will be going to a particular charity.

You will often find that people who would not normally attend a party will because of the charity connection.

You may find a hostess that is involved with a charity already, and would like you to hold a party for her and donate a portion of your commission to her named charity. She is likely to be known for her charity work, and the connection with her promoting your products will open the door to other people for you that you would not normally be able to contact.

At the party you could take a popular product and 'raffle' it as an added fund-raiser. This idea has been used in the past, and is an excellent way to raise money. All you do is take a popular product and sell tickets, and whoever has the winning ticket, takes the gift.

There are many many more ideas that you can use, and as long as you remember that these specific funds raised are for charity, and that you will be asked again to assist, fund-raising parties are great fun and will help to promote your business locally. Sometimes, the local press get involved in fund-raising events, and this is an area worth exploring.

Party Plan is a wonderful way of earning extra money, and meeting new people. Women who have children find this a wonderful way to contribute to the household income, and yet still have ample time for their family. The parties are either during the day, held around school hours, or early evening, when the husband is able to have time on his own with the family. It is an ideal business that you run yourself, and you do not have to worry about building a network in quite the same way as you might with an MLM company.

However, if you like the concept of Party Plan, and the company that you are with, or are about to join, has products that would lend itself to being marketed via Party Plan, then you need to read on to discover how to recruit people to help build your organisation...

Learning Points From Chapter Seven:

1.   I understand how the Party Plan system works, and if possible, I have adapted some of the ideas to fit my own business.

2.   Where possible, I have contacted someone who is actively involved with Party Plan and observed them doing a 'party'. Where possible, I have used ideas to further successfully promote my business.

3.   I fully understand why it is important to maintain regular contact with hostesses after the party in order to secure future business.

4.   Where possible, I have shared the Party Plan ideas with my network.

Notes:

_____

_____

_____

_____

Chapter Eight

How Many People?

The basis of network marketing is simply to sell the product yourself and recruit others to do the same. That is to multiply yourself through the efforts of others. Think of how much easier it would be to have fifty people sell your products, and recruit new distributors. Ideally you will earn a percentage from each of them, and the amount or percentage that you will be paid is dependent upon you as an individual reaching the different levels in the company.

Your success will be determined by your consistency and persistence, by your desire to succeed.

"Success is achieved when you deserve it, not when you need it"

When you have decided on the company you want to join, and you have had the basic training from your sponsor for the marketing plan, you will want to invite others to join you in your new venture. Alternatively, you may have been with your company for some time now and believe the opportunity is too good for others to miss!

What do you do first?

The list

There are two types of people – the ones you know and the ones you don't. Talk to the ones you know first. The first thing that you need to do is make a list of the people that you know, or if you have followed the earlier chapters refer to the list you have already compiled. You will probably have heard this before, maybe dozens of times, and are now groaning and saying "Not again!"

But the compilation of the list does work, and here's why:

First of all, if you take the time to write down the names, it is in part a commitment to yourself and your sponsor that you are somewhat serious about the business opportunity presented to you. Secondly, the list will help your memory to think of all sorts of people that you come across. Not everyone you can think of to put on this list will come to you in an instant, but rather over a period of time you will add to the list.

The list starts off with those names of people you know now and remember, then gradually you add the names of people that you had forgotten about, and this will be a gradual addition to the list. (Please refer to Chapter One where the process of list creation is also covered and will greatly benefit you.) People you put on the list will trigger your memory for names that you had forgotten. Then the list will be continually updated because every day you will come across new people that may be interested either in the business opportunity or to purchase the products.

Some people have a real problem with this list idea, and some sponsors will insist that the list be done immediately and given to them to contact, but if you take the view that the list is merely a record over a period of time of those people you have spoken to, and those you have not spoken to, with notes as to what took place during any conversation, you will get further with the concept.

When you think about it, it is necessary to have some form of record-keeping for your business, as you need to know who you have talked to, what the outcome was, when to contact them again if appropriate, and those still waiting to be contacted.

Who do you put on this list? We have mentioned this earlier, but it is important to emphasise this again, make a list of everyone you know. Don't prejudge, just write down who you know. When the list is complete, categorise the people into the following categories and place a tick beside the person's name:

- Those who live within one hour's travelling time

- Successful people

- Entrepreneurs and risk takers

- Those dissatisfied with their present income

- Those dissatisfied with their current job

- People who own their own business

- High credibility with others

The people with the most ticks are the ones to contact first!

Call and arrange to see them as soon as is convenient. Start *now*, don't put it off.

Remember, when you start contacting people the momentum is created, everyone gets swept along with it. People like to associate themselves with successful people, and if you are successful, people will be attracted to you and want to join your organisation. The more times that you are in front of people talking about the products and the opportunity, the more opportunity you have of expanding your business, not only in terms of recruits, but also product sales. Remember: See the People, See the People, See the People!

When you build your business quickly, and with success, you create momentum and a sense of urgency, and this can make the ride to the top that much easier!

Using the products

It is important to have your recruits actually use the products that the company offer. If the recruit has no belief in the products, it will be difficult for them to sincerely promote the product to customers. Customers know when you don't use the products!

Think about it. You are looking for recruits to promote a new slimming product, you are thirty pounds overweight, the recruit has known you for ten years, and you say you have a wonderful new product, guaranteed to help shed unwanted weight. What do you think the prospective recruit will think? Does the product work? How can I sell a product that doesn't work, and how can I find new recruits?

Then you get asked if you are actually using the product yourself, and you answer 'no'. It will give no credibility to the product, company or you that there is any belief in the product.

Now, on the other hand, same situation, you are overweight, the prospective recruit has known you for years, and knows how you have struggled to lose the weight. You arrive on their doorstep excited about a new product on the market; you are using the product, and achieving results, which they can see, and you are looking for people to join the business with you. You are more likely to get a positive response from this situation than the previous one! Why make life difficult? "How hard do you want it to be?" Use the products and be a product of the product, and your recruiting will be much easier. You cannot teach that which you are not prepared to do yourself. So make sure that the recruits that you bring into the business also use the products, just as you do!

This situation can be the same for a variety of products. If you don't use the products, and your enthusiasm for the product is not there, you will find it very difficult to build a network.

What do you say?

What do you say to your prospective recruits? Many established companies have a very good recruiting approach that works well for their products, and can be a demonstration with dialogue about the success or uniqueness of the product, or it can be a leaflet or brochure that you need to read, then follow up with a visit, or, the easiest way, is to have a presentation that you are comfortable with that lasts just one minute. Make it short, sharp and punchy. If the prospective recruit says 'yes', then you can go further, supply them with the tools – a book, the video or a tape of the opportunity available to them. The full presentation, time permitting, could be up to half an hour, depending on the product, marketing plan and interest of the prospect.

The one-minute presentation is a very brief check to determine the seriousness of the prospect for the business opportunity. The opening questions can be very simple, for example, "Are you seriously interested in earning extra income?" If the answer is 'yes', ask what have they tried before, and why it didn't work. Take the information that you have been given, and give a very brief summary of your success, and end with a phrase similar to this: "...and you could build a network like mine too! When would you like to discuss this further? Monday evening or Tuesday morning?"

Make the appointment and sit down with the person and show them how the marketing plan will work for them to build a network of people. Remember to 'keep it simple', don't complicate it, just show how it will work for them, and highlight only how it worked for you.

People's perception of how the business works is based on how you bring them into it. Most people don't want you sit and talk to them for two or three hours. This situation will ultimately lead to the potential recruit saying that they do not have the time for the business opportunity you are presenting to them.

The above one-minute presentation can also be used if you are promoting the products, and you want to determine if the person really does want to purchase your product. All that you need to do is structure your initial question around the product that you are marketing. If it is a weight-loss product, you could start by asking them if they are seriously interested in losing weight. If it is cosmetics, you could ask if they are seriously interested in purchasing a skin-care range that will be suited to their particular skin type. If the answer is 'yes', then your next question should be to ask what they have previously tried, followed by why it didn't work. Take the negative from what they have said, and turn it around to a positive about the product that you have to offer. For example, if you are marketing a weight-loss product that will allow the person to eat small meals, and the prospective customer has tried a product that meant all meals were replaced by tablets, what you should say is that your product will assist them in their weight-loss programme, and still allow them the pleasure of having small, regular meals.

The importance of training a new recruit

You need to train your new recruit as quickly as possible, because until then, you haven't properly sponsored someone. You need to assist them to make their first few sales, help them to sponsor their first distributors and show them how to hold meetings. All this is accomplished by training the recruit from the moment they say yes to the business opportunity that you are presenting them. Training is ongoing, and your responsibility as the sponsor is to ensure that there is training provided by you, and that the recruit is aware of any training provided by the company.

When you are recruiting, you need to be available to teach and train them how the marketing plan works, how the products work, and the selling features of the products. This will not come to a new recruit instantly, but over a period of time. Remember how long it may have taken you to attain an acceptable level of competence!

The best way to help the recruit gain all of this knowledge is in the form of training sessions. When and how you do them is up to you, but it is important that there is some form of training, and that there is some regularity with the training.

Where do you get all the information needed to train your new recruit? Ideally, you are attending the company training sessions, talking to other distributors, and reading books, just like the one you are reading now! It is your responsibility to ensure your network has as much knowledge and information about the products and the MLM industry as is possible. You must however remember, whatever information you obtain, and relay to your network to follow, you must be prepared to do yourself!

One on one training can be appropriate when you have 'signed up' the recruit, and they need to know a few basics to get them on their way.

If the product is a consumable, give them directions on how to use the product, and then have them tell you how they will take it. This clears up any misunderstanding when what you think you said is not what the person thought you said!

The first step of the marketing plan also needs to be dealt with. What is the first level of remuneration that they need to know? Quite simply, how many widgets need to be sold to customers to reach a certain amount of volume, or how many widgets need to be sold to result in the amount of Retail Profit that the recruit told you was needed (Refer to Chapter Two for more on a marketing plan).

From a recruiting view, how many recruits does the person need to have, each doing a certain amount of volume to create a group volume, and a wholesale profit for the recruit?

At the close of this discussion, the recruit needs to know when the next training will take place, what time and where and what the content will be. It is important for your new recruit to understand that they are encouraged to bring along their own new recruits to these training sessions. This would be a good time to give the new recruit several brochures for recruiting, products and any publications from the company that they can talk to people about.

It is a far better use of your time to train a group of people at one time than to do numerous one on ones and spend a considerable amount of time travelling to each, and repeating yourself. Your enthusiasm will eventually wane, and your recruit or prospect will notice! If your potential new recruit sees the lack of enthusiasm, they may pass the opportunity by as not being sufficiently stimulating, rewarding or exciting!

When you have recruited someone new to the business, you need to keep in touch to encourage them to talk to people, and use the products. Only by constant contact, imparting positive information on a regular basis, will your recruits start to succeed.

Your recruits need to have faith in you as their upline/sponsor. Remember, they have no reason to believe you could mislead them because you won't make money until you help them to make money first. Therefore, you need to attend the training events, and you need to take the business seriously.

The phone call

The new recruit should have a phone call from you ideally at the end of their first full day as a distributor. You want them to tell you what they had done, and how successful did they feel the day had gone. If there are any problems, or misunderstanding of instructions, now is the time to find out, and set things back on the correct track.

The new recruit will be faced with a number of 'no's from his prospect list, and he will need encouragement to continue on. We have all experienced the negatives, and sometimes they can start to wear us down, so you need to be aware of this with your new recruit. If they are down, build them back up with positive encouragement.

When you have got past the first day, regular contact needs to be maintained in order to continue the ongoing training programme with the recruit. Each time that you speak to the recruit, give them a little bit more information, either about the marketing plan or the products.

Check to make sure what you have previously discussed is understood, and the plans are being carried out. Check on the success to date. If there had been a 'no' from someone, discuss how to try and prevent the situation from happening again.

The new recruit needs to know that there is the help and support from you and the person who sponsored you, if they are available. Also, the recruit needs to know that there is also help and support direct from the company. If there is a distributor relations telephone number available, make sure they have it.

The Testimonial Book

There are a number of companies who encourage their distributors to create a Testimonial Book, and if properly put together and used, this can be an invaluable tool for any recruit for both retailing and recruiting.

What is a Testimonial Book?

The book is simply a folder with plastic pockets, and is used as a 'Presentation Book' where the pockets at the front contain information about the company, how long they have been in business, and the current annual sales. People like to see established companies, and if the sales figures are there, people can see the success of the company.

The next section will contain some information about the products. The feature of the product is mentioned, but the benefit of what the product can do for someone is of more interest to a customer. The left page could show the product, and the right page highlight what it has done for someone. Several pages like this, highlighting different products should be inserted. Ideally, one of the stories should be your own, and some of the stories should be about people that are either your customers or distributors. To be able to talk about people that are local, and that are known to you, will support the fact that the products in fact do what they are supposed to do.

The third section should contain stories about the income that can be generated from the company. You want to show a spread of income – not just the high earners who are few and far between. You want to be able to show some part-time distributors – a variance of ages is also important. Ultimately you want to show a spread of people of all ages, promoting the business opportunity, both full-time and part-time, and also people who are only part-time and are perhaps only retailing the products. If you have any stories about couples who promote the business part-time, they should also be included.

The reason that you need such a spread is that you don't know who you are going to come across in the promoting of your business. If someone can relate to the information that you have included in your book, they are more likely to say 'yes' to you.

Not everyone that you come across will have aspirations to make a fortune with your company. Many will just want a part-time income that suits the hours they are willing to devote to the business. If you think logically, the more part-timers you have, generating a consistent amount of volume each month, is exactly what you need within your network.

Consistency is the key to building a solid foundation. If the foundation of your business is solid, and based on consistently retailing the products and talking to people, then your business will develop. A lot will depend on your ability to also consistently retail the products and talk to people. People look up for guidance rather than at themselves in the mirror. The example that you set therefore *must be the best that you are able to do.*

Knowing what the recruit wants from the business

When you are recruiting people into your organisation, you need to know what it is that they want to get out of their involvement with the company. Is it more money, meeting new people, they like the products and want the best discount possible, or do they want the challenge of something new in their life?

Each person will come into the business for their own reasons, and they are not necessarily the same reasons why you joined. Don't worry, if they are committed to join and obtain an element of success that is relevant to them, work with them as best you can and share with them all the information that you can. If you are seen to be involved in the development of your network, each distributor will follow and do the same, thus strengthening the foundation.

It is important to note that the reasons you joined the company may not be the same reasons that would make the prospective agent/distributor say 'yes' to you for the opportunity. Everyone will join for different reasons, similar perhaps, but quite often different, so do not assume people will join for the reasons you did. Remember the questioning and listening skills covered earlier in Chapter Four. To ensure that you do not find yourself in this trap, just make sure that you ask the prospective agent/distributor very early on what it is they wish to achieve with the company. From there, you can relate to the Testimonial or Presentation Book you have compiled, and highlight other instances that are of a similar nature to your prospect. When they can see others that they think are similar to themselves, it will help them to decide in a positive manner towards the business opportunity.

When you are recruiting, do not fall into the trap of signing up everyone. There will be some people who you do not want as agents/distributors or that you do not want to be involved with, possibly due to a clash of personalities, a severe concern over their commitment or just a lack of confidence in their ability to perform.

So who do you recruit? Basically anybody you come across that is ethical, has a genuine need or desire to achieve certain goals from being involved with the company and ultimately someone who will listen to and act upon receipt of good training. You should also consider buying them a copy of this book to really get them off to a good start!

By working closely with your network, you will get to know them, and work with them to help them achieve their objectives.

Building your network is a constant task. You will lose people because of family or other work commitments, they may move and not want to be involved for a period of time while they settle in, or they may just lose interest.

If your new recruit has lost interest very quickly, you may not be doing your job as the upline sponsor to the best of your ability. Why did they lose interest? Was it because you did not keep in close contact with them, or teach and train them about the products that your company has to offer? Maybe, your training and opportunity meetings were not lively or informative. Nobody likes to attend a boring meeting!

So if you have a recruit who loses interest very quickly, step back and look at how you promote yourself, your network and the company. You may need to make some changes. You need to ask yourself if you are conducting exciting and stimulating meetings. Do people come back with new recruits time and time again, or do they show up once, leave before the end and never contact you again? If it is someone who leaves after a long period of time, examine the circumstances more closely, because you may in part be responsible.

Remember, when recruiting, you need a balance of part-time and full-time distributors because each will operate their business differently.

Many part-time people will never achieve the higher levels of the marketing plan, and as such stay at a lower rate of discount, and you benefit from this in the wholesale profit you earn, but also from the volume that the recruit creates that will form part of your Personal Group Volume. This group generally tends to be easy to work with, as they have limited time, and are not going to need much support in building their small businesses.

On the other hand, you also need to recruit the full-time distributor who wants to earn a more substantial income, and has more time to devote to the business. These people will want to have your attention constantly, and we deal with how to handle this in Chapter Eleven. With this recruit they will, with your training, become more independent, and become a part of your overall organisation. The more people that you have in this situation, the bigger your organisation will grow.

Advertising for a recruit

Newspaper advertising is a very passive way of advertising for anything. You are solely dependent upon someone buying a newspaper, reading your advert and picking up the telephone and asking you to sponsor them into your business. From experience, this very rarely happens. Why?

It is rare because you will not be the only advert in your local paper. There are likely to be other people from your company advertising and also people from other companies. Why should you be the one picked to sponsor the potential recruit? Admittedly you may obtain a few responses but what you are looking for will be a great deal more than this.

In some countries there are rules and regulations in place that prohibit the placing of adverts for recruits, and sometimes customers. Some countries will allow you to place adverts, but the rules and regulations are very stringent about what you can say. Whatever country you are in, you need to be aware of these rules and regulations.

Let's focus on the need for a recruiting advert. If you have your list of people, you should be busy enough with that. Referrals from the list will come to you. Customers will refer more customers to you, and some will become distributors. Why place an advert?

We are not saying don't place an advert, what we are saying is don't use it as the only means of recruiting.

There are many types of adverts that work, from the short, sharp advert to the 'laundry list' advert that is very expensive. Everyone is different, and different adverts work for different people. It is important to remember that all adverts will cost money, and generally new recruits are looking at the business opportunity to make money, not spend it. So, work from the list for the first months.

Taking calls from an advert can be very demotivating for a new recruit. Many people will call adverts in the hope of finding the 'get rich quick' scheme, or the scheme that pays you to do no work at all! You will get plenty of 'no's from adverts when you do not fulfil their expectations of money for no work.

With adverts you have no personal contact, unless you are able to have the person come along to your next opportunity meeting. Even then, you have no idea of the person's background, and exactly what they are looking for. They do not know you, therefore your 'Testimonial' doesn't mean the same to them as it would to others who know you.

Adverts are a numbers game. You receive lots of calls, spend hours on the phone 'pitching' your company and the opportunity, chase people up to attend the next opportunity meeting, only to find that out of thirty phone calls received, one person shows up, and the only reason they came along was because there wasn't much on television that night to interest them!

You could be mistaken for thinking we do not recommend promoting the concept of local advertising for your network. Any legal avenue from which to source new recruits must be considered; all we are emphasising here is for you to ensure the main focus of any distributor, new or existing, is not solely based around their dependence on local advertising.

We have only discussed local advertising here because the next section is about international sponsoring, and this is when advertising can be useful. Again, it should not be used as the only means of obtaining international recruits.

In summary, local adverts have their place, but it would be best not to direct your new recruits to the advertising section of their local newspaper as the place to start building their business. MLM is a word-of-mouth business, built primarily on personal contact, not only for promoting the products, but in recruiting people into the business. Keep it simple and easy for your new distributors; after all, "How hard do you want it to be – for them?"

International sponsoring

International sponsoring is really no different from sponsoring someone within your country who lives quite a distance from you. You keep in contact by telephone or by post, both with company material and your own literature (newsletter). Modern technology may also allow you to maintain contact via faxes or e-mail!

The main difference is that the products and marketing plan may slightly differ from what is in place in your country, so you need to use material from the recruit's country.

How do you get international recruits? The best approach is the 'Who do you know?' in whatever country you are looking at recruiting in. Generally, if you ask your customers or your down-line who they know, in a particular country, they will give you the name of a relative. Personal contact is the best form of recruiting, and it should be the focus of your international recruiting.

However, there may be the opportunity to place adverts in the local papers, and you may find this is an 'added bonus' to you. First, make sure through your company that the adverts conform to the rules and regulations of the country. From experience, placing international adverts is costly, and most people who are comfortable with this exercise have a considerable amount of MLM experience. Ideally, place the adverts and then go to the country and spend some time actively recruiting. Don't expect the adverts alone to build your international business.

If you are contemplating recruiting in another country, obtain as many contacts first from your downline, customers and people who may have said 'no' to the opportunity, but may know someone in another country who may be interested.

One of the wonders of modern technology today is the computer with its ability to bring the world even closer. If you have the facil-ities, go on the Internet and see what transpires! But again remember, don't focus on advertising as the only means of promoting your business.

Many companies now are expanding worldwide, and as such there is a tremendous opportunity for someone to sponsor in another country, and when appropriate, visit that country and assist the recruit with the promotion of his business.

Be aware, you *must not* sponsor anyone until the company has officially opened to trade in that country! To sponsor before this time could result in the company being declined approval to operate in that country because of local legislation. You can, however, talk to people about the opportunity that will be coming, and have them start to put their list of names together.

Literature about the products and the opportunity could also be sent, provided that they do not contravene the rules of the country. Product generally should not be sent, but it's best to ask your company direct what their guidelines are. When the country is ready to conduct business, there will be local literature and distributor kits available, and you would be advised to have a set so that you are aware of any changes in the company's method of operation in that country.

There is a benefit to you in international sponsoring – in a brand new country for your company to operate in there will be tremendous opportunities to develop a large and productive network very quickly. In addition, you can get paid in the currency of the country that you have the recruits in, and you have the ability to travel!

When you are first dealing with a recruit in another country, it is important to keep in touch with them. The company and possibly the concept are new to the country, and the recruit may experience some negative feedback. Just like your local recruit, keep in touch as often as you can, provide as much support and encouragement as possible, and supply them with a copy of this book to really give them the greatest chance of success!

You will need to teach and train your network, and be able to motivate them to talk to people and use the products at every opportunity. How do you monitor your business? How do you know what is happening in your organisation? You need to be able to read the signs...

Learning Points From Chapter Eight:

1. I am continuing to compile and categorise my list of people to contact.

2. I train my network to compile and categorise their own lists of people to contact.

3. I have developed a short presentation about the company and products, and I regularly have the opportunity to practise.

4. At training sessions, I regularly work with my network to create a short presentation for them that they are comfortable with.

5. When I recruit someone, I contact them after the first day, and regularly thereafter.

6. I have started to create a 'Testimonial Book' from my own stories and those of my downline and upline.

7. Do you know what level of success each of your downline want to achieve? Do you actively assist them in achieving their goals?

8. If you use advertising, are you aware of how effective it is? How do you monitor the success of the adverts?

Notes:

_____

_____

_____

_____

_____

_____

_____

_____

Chapter Nine

Knowing When And How To Fix It

This chapter is ideal for anyone within the structure of the network marketing plan system. You can be a new recruit who needs to know and understand the need of monitoring, or the more experienced networker who has a large organisation that is spread across the country.

This could even be of benefit to the company management when there are a number of people who are responsible for the smooth running of their department.

Do you know what is going on within your organisation before anything happens, or do you just sit and anticipate that something is going to go wrong, and deal with it then?

Do you drive a car? Have you been driving for quite some time? Can you remember when you first started to drive, and how you were very careful about what you did every time you got in your car to drive? You got in the car, checked your mirrors, checked your seat belt, checked the car was in neutral before starting and made sure your hands were in the 'proper' position on the wheel.

Did you also regularly check your speed whilst driving and also other things like the fuel and oil levels?

What do you do now? Jump in, turn the key and speed away, hoping others notice you and give you the manoeuvring room you need!!

Do you ever take the time to check under the bonnet (hood) now, or take a look at the gauges on the dashboard?

An interesting discovery – if you do not check the running of the car at regular intervals, something is going to go wrong! And when it does how inconvenient and expensive it can be! Also, the better the performance of the car, the more closely you have to watch the controls.

What has the running of a car got to do with the running of your own businesses? Actually, not very much, aside from the fact that you might need the car to get to work each day. But more important than that, in effect the running of a car is very similar to the running of your business.

Are all businesses the same?

Not all cars are the same, and not all businesses are the same. Just look at the local businesses near where you live, and you will realise that they are all different. They also have different philosophies, different products. Even those who you target as agents or distributors and customers can differ. The same is true about cars. Not all are the same!

If you have ever driven a high-performance car you will know that there is a difference in driving a Ford Escort to a Mercedes 200SLK to driving a Ferrari. With a Ferrari, you have to carefully watch the controls, you need to pay more attention to the speed you are travelling at (it can be deceptive!), the sounds of the engine, the high revs (red zone) that will indicate you need to gauge when to change the gears. You need to pay attention to the petrol, some use more than others and you don't want to run out.

Even the operation of the clutch and the brakes are different.

If you drive the car and don't pay attention to the sounds of the engine, and what the gauges say on the dashboard, you are in for some problems. And then again, at the next level up. It's a very different experience driving a Formula One racing car compared to a Porsche, Mercedes, Ferrari and a Ford. You have to be more conscious of what the engine is saying to you. If you change gears too late, the warnings are there. If you don't ensure the oil and water is put in, the warnings come up – the needle goes to the 'red' warning you of possible trouble. If you drive too much on the 'red' you are asking for trouble – breakdown or component failure.

The 'Danger Gauge'

We are not suggesting that you should spend all of your time watching the gauges and controls of your car for that will surely result in an accident!! Naturally you also need to watch where you are going and other road users and take into account other events going on around you.

But keeping a watchful eye on the gauges and controls is crucial to the continuing long-term reliability of your vehicle, and also the reduction in expensive repair bills!

The same is true of your business. If you run your business knowing something will go wrong, but you are not sure what, or even when, you just hope that you can deal with it when it happens. Do you feel that this is the most effective way to run your business and how much control do you have?

The need for contact

Maybe you are the type of person that is always too busy to return or take the calls from your network. Maybe there are some distributors that you would rather not talk to. But sometimes you don't speak to certain people because of the drain that they can be to your time. They may think that they deserve your time, but in reality they do not.

You could fit into the category of someone who is of the opinion that no contact is good. You maybe did not have the help and support of the person who sponsored you, and you take the view that if you had no help, and got to where you are today, then your network can just get on with it without your help.

This could be a drastic mistake because the very network that you are depending on to generate the monthly volume sales may one day quit because there was no help or support, or worse still, they were made to feel that they were only there as a means of generating more commission for you.

The problem could be that you are unsure of your ability to talk to your network. You may have had a job where there was a lack of people contact, and therefore you are unsure of your ability to get the message across to new customers or recruits. The problem may be further complicated by the fact that your sponsor may be someone who is constantly dealing with people, and has a considerable amount of experience with the company, and you feel unable to match their skills.

Deliver the message

Don't worry. It is not the messenger that is the issue, it is the message. If you use the products and have had results, tell people. If you have used the products and earned money, tell people. The people that you speak to will decide for themselves what they want to do. If you are honest and sincere, it will show.

This will help someone to decide what they want to do, probably based on the fact that they feel they could do a presentation better than you.

It is important to remember that it is not necessary to be highly skilled, just act professionally (be honest), do your follow up, follow through with your plan and build on your growing reputation. This will firmly start you along a route which could be called, your very own *pathway to success.*

If you are in a management position within a Direct Sales organisation, and you feel that your business is run this way, do you think that the network that are promoting your products might do the same with the way they run their businesses? Who and what is checking this for you? Sometimes the example that you set is not the best example for a distributor to run his own business.

You should make yourself available to handle the calls of your network and try to keep in touch with them. Maybe not phone them all every week, but possibly with a newsletter, or attend the corporate functions and try and ensure that as many people from your organisation also attend, and you make a point of meeting with them.

If you are watching the controls on a car, you can gauge what is going to happen, just as if you are watching the running of your company, you can gauge what is going to happen. You are then in a position to foresee what problems if any might occur.

You can also project how well you are doing, as it is important to be able to project the sales for the coming months so that the manufacturing can be geared to meet the anticipated needs and both you and your upline (management?) are aware of the future potential business.

The controls

There are two main controls you need to monitor in your business.

The first control that you need to look at with your business is the amount of *literature* that is being purchased and distributed. It is not enough that literature is being purchased. You must be certain the distributor has taken it from the boot of the car, the bottom of the cupboard or from underneath the bed and given it to someone who shows a genuine interest. Long after the distributor has left, the paper stays and then can be referred to by the potential customer. By including a contact phone number on the literature, the distributor or agent can be contacted again in the future for orders.

What is included in literature? It could be product brochures, opportunity leaflets, videos depicting products, marketing plans or just generally about the company. It can also be the new distributor packs, which will include the enrolment forms for new members to join.

Ideally, your distributors should be taught to purchase literature, maybe on a monthly basis, and ensure that the literature is used in that month. Re-order again the next month, and the month after that, making sure that you use the current month's supply. Why? Because there may be changes in prices, new products being introduced and products being deleted. Do you want literature circulated that is almost a year out of date? How professional does that make you look?

What about the brochure on the company? How good is the image of the company portrayed if there are coffee stains on the cover, the edges are curled up, and the brochure is two seasons out of date?

How much literature should be purchased? That depends on a number of things, ranging from funds available, time available (their commitment) to promote the company and how they plan to promote the products and the income potential. Also, will the new recruit be full-time or part-time?

How much time are they willing to devote to this business? You may also want to ask them how they plan to contact potential customers.

If they are looking at recruiting, you need to know if the potential recruits will be local or at a distance. The amount of literature that will be needed will be greater if the potential recruits are at a distance, as you will want to ensure that they receive as much information about the products and the business opportunity as possible.

How much money?

Let's start at the beginning – available funds. You have a new recruit that is going to place an order for a certain amount of product that will be used for their own consumption, and have a few products on hand for when they are talking to people and someone says yes they want to purchase the item. You need to determine how much the person is comfortable investing, and enlighten them on the need to purchase literature to professionally promote the company.

Maybe 10% of the funds available should go to literature. It is difficult to say exactly how much should be invested, but whatever the amount, it should reflect on the comfort level of the person doing the investing, and what method they are going to use to promote the company.

If someone is going to promote the company and look for recruits that are out of the area, say their home town, then the literature that is purchased should be enough to promote the products, and the income potential. Proof that the product lives up to its expectations should also be included – the testimonial. Many companies now that deal with weight-loss and nutrition have a comprehensive library of stories that are available upon request. If you are thinking of getting involved with a company that does not have a consumable product, make sure that you have proof of the company's guarantee that the product will do what is stated. Again, this is usually company supplied.

The need for quality literature

The need to distribute literature to potential customers and distributors in order to recruit and retain is something that most companies are aware of when setting the prices for the literature.

Quite a number of companies absorb a high proportion of the costs because they know that they will increase profits and recover losses on printing by the sale of products or the joining of a new recruit. If the price is low enough, the distributors will order in bulk.

What will sometimes happen however, is that the cost of literature is so expensive that distributors start to circulate 'home-grown' literature – fifth generation photocopies, poor scribbled notes photocopied, outdated and obsolete information, and occasionally, outrageous testimonials both for the income potential and what the product will or will not do. These are not activities to be encouraged!

We know of several companies that will allow the distributor to buy a certain number of 'distributor kits' and receive one for free. This is a good marketing tool for the company, because the distributors invariably buy in bulk, and then recruit because they want a quick return on their investment, and they consider the 'free' kit as extra profit.

The bulk purchase of kits and literature should be dealt with on a month to month basis, that is, invest what money you are comfortable with, then add just a bit more to encourage you to exceed your targets. If you do not do this, but merely stay within your 'comfort zone' then you may never become a key person in the organisation, and many people that you recruit will surpass you in their network growth because they were willing to invest that little bit more in funds for the extra literature, and also invest that little bit more time in talking to people about the opportunity available to them. You need to push yourself that little bit further in order to attain personal growth.

If you order, for example, one company video, and distribute it to several potential recruits, over a period of time, that is good, but if you invested in ten videos, and did the same thing, then you would have the potential to have your business grow ten times more quickly.

This brings us to a question that we are asked, and many others have asked their sponsors, "I can't afford to buy all that literature from the company, so could I buy one and copy it, then distribute the literature and build my business that way?"

The standard reply could be, "I don't know about that, all I know is that I purchase the professional company literature and I recruit new people every month". Or, "I don't know about that, all I know is that I purchase the product literature from the company, and I sold lots of product last month".

An important point for the upline person to remember, is that the amount available by your new recruit for product should also include a portion for literature. You do not make any commission on the sale of literature, but it is a short-term idea to think that if there is only a certain amount of funds available, then product alone should be ordered so that you can obtain the maximum amount of commission from that person.

Long-term business building, which is the way successful networkers build their business, would advise that a percentage of available funds be invested in literature. Again, the more literature circulating, the more likely you will be to pick up the 'yes's from prospects.

There are several useful phrases that are used by many people in network marketing, and you should try and remember them, especially when looking to sell more products or recruit new members; here are a few:

"Where literature goes, product flows"
"When you pay money for print, you can print money"

Try and encourage your network to adopt these sayings, and follow what they say. It is important to understand the reason why company literature is so important and, how when used effectively, it can help to build your long-term business and increase the success you achieve.

We don't want you to think that only company literature should go out. What we are saying is company literature is the first choice – it is professional, and the cost will probably be minimal for what you are getting. Sometimes though, a distributor can put together promotional material that is of an excellent quality, and fits the needs of how they are going to go about retailing or recruiting.

If this situation should arise, you need to contact your company and give them a copy of what you want to do, and obtain their approval before you start to distribute the literature – just in case you breach a particular code of practice or certain legal requirements are not met.

When your company gives guidelines of literature that you are able to duplicate and use, please make sure that you stay within the guidelines recommended by the company.

We earlier mentioned there are two controls you need to watch, and the next control (gauge) that you need to keep a very close eye on is your *Marketing Plan Profit.*

From a company view, the management know the plan, they are aware of what the profit is, or could be if the cash flow projections become a reality! But, does the network of people that are out there promoting the products understand how the plan can work best for them?

We have been told repeatedly that the vast majority of the distributors do not understand the marketing plan of their company and especially how they can make the plan work best for them. As a result many 'lost' opportunities (and money!) have occurred.

The marketing plan should be broken into three sections: Retail Profit, Wholesale Profit and Loyalty Bonuses. (See Chapter Two for more details.)

Which one should you keep a check on? Should it be the *Retail Profit,* because that is an indication that there is an increase in retail customers, who will eventually re-order, and possibly become future distributors? Well, what this provides is an indication that there will be an increase in the future for retail sales, which means an increase in company profit. This can be reflected in the Cash Flow Projections that you compile and which help you forecast future sales.

If you keep a record of your sales, and where they come from, it will assist you in the future planning of your business. For example, if you know that every time a new product has been launched, and you introduced it to your existing customers, that your profit increases steadily each time, this may assist you in planning future orders when products are introduced.

What about the *Loyalty Bonus* that is on offer? Most companies have a proportion of distributors who are working 'full-time'. These distributors are actively recruiting and retailing the products. Their incomes are generally high, and they have several distributors in their organisation who are also working on a 'full-time' basis. You know that you can depend upon them and their downline ordering a certain amount of product every month, and their bonus cheques are usually consistent. What this provides is an indication of their level of commitment to the organisation, the fact that they are building a business that will generate an income for them and you!

Neither of these sections will tell you what will happen with your business. All that they will do is tell you the results of what has happened in the past, good or bad. They are not a *real* indication of what *will* happen in the future. They are history, a result of possibly a new product, a competition or maybe the sale of a particular product related to the recent festive season. The figures could help you to decide to do something if they are lower than anticipated!

They are like the history of your car, the regular services carried out and stored in the service log book. It tells you how many miles you have gone between services, it tells you what you have had replaced. It tells you what has happened, not what is going to happen.

The section that will, however, indicate to you what will happen in your business is the *Wholesale Volume Profit (WVP)*. The more product that is ordered reflects on how much more business there will be in the coming months.

The volume that is created in your network each month will increase because as product is ordered, it will be sold, and sales will result in referrals and repeat business. An increase in the volume will also indicate that there is active recruiting taking place. Each distributor needs product for personal use, and their aim with the business opportunity is to generate additional income, therefore they will promote the company and the products, thus increasing their bank account.

A simple example of a network is shown below and you need to study this in order to understand how the Wholesale Volume Profit will increase:

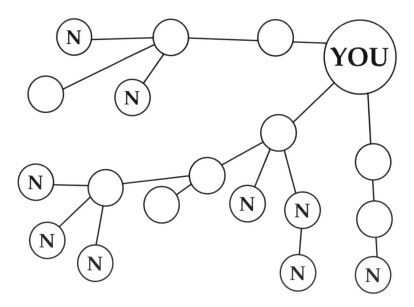

N = new distributor

From the diagram, can you see how this person at the top will increase his Wholesale Volume Profit in the coming months?

The WVP needs to be viewed as a daily cash flow. Most people will say that they are working on their network/recruiting/retail sales, and at the end of the month the figures will be up. This is *wrong*. It may happen, but usually does not because other things get in the way.

The need for adjustment

Ideally you and your agents/distributors should monitor the WVP weekly. Set targets, as it helps to enforce productivity, and you will be guided by the level of commitment of the new recruit. The sales of this week must meet or exceed the WVP of the previous week. If it does not, then there needs to be an 'adjustment' to what is being done. You need to find out why something is not right.

Just like your car, from time to time it may need to have a slight 'tweaking' or adjustment to the engine or additional air put in the tyres – minor *but* important adjustments to ensure it maintains its performance.

Therefore whilst the adjustments for your agent/distributor may not be anything major to you, just a minor adjustment, to the distributor it may be major. Such adjustments are very important and necessary to avoid a future sales slump.

It is easier to 'adjust' than make any major changes, and many times people will let things carry on for a long period of time, and rather than be faced with the realisation that there is a need to correct the situation, to make 'major' changes, they will invariably quit.

You need to find out why the distributor is not maintaining the usual level of sales. Many factors could be the cause, from the sales approach that they are using or their inability to ask for a positive answer when doing a recruiting or product presentation. The distributor may even have heard someone do their presentation differently than their own, and they are trying to duplicate that person. Good idea, but maybe the approach is just not suited to the individual.

This is when they need to go back to what they had been previously doing, if it was providing results. If the system they previously used had always worked quite well, then perhaps they don't change it, or as the saying goes;

"If it ain't broke, don't fix it!"

If you have kept a sharp eye on the running of the business, you know the sales figures, then you should be able to spot when you need to make these 'adjustments'.

If you let a potential problem continue to the end of the month, you take your concentration off what you are doing, and you are setting the scene for problems in the coming months. Not only will you be faced with making up the loss of the previous month, but you now have the sales target for the entire month that is coming up. You go 'off-track' and this is when your distributors can easily become 'de-motivated' and go into a slump. You may agree that this is not a good way to start a month!

If you start from a negative position, you have a tremendous amount of work to do to make up the loss in sales, and also re-motivate the organisation to make up the loss of sales!

Going into a slump can be the easier option than trying to get back on track after an unnecessarily long period of time. Take control immediately, make the minor adjustments, and carry on.

This will help in reducing the possibility of any network 'slump'.

Many components make a car work, much like a company – there are people and departments – but the one key component in a car is the 'distributor', much like the company that you have chosen, or will choose; without the distributors, it will not work.

Just like driving a car, watch the controls, watch what you are doing, and if you have to change gears to go up or down a hill, do so. By watching the controls of your business, you gain more confidence in the ability of the network to retail, recruit and promote your organisation because you have been able to learn their strengths and weaknesses, thus enabling you to help guide them through the necessary stages to become a key member of your organisation.

Once you understand the need to actively and regularly monitor the controls, and make the necessary adjustments, your success will be a formality. Only the extent of your success is in question, and here is where you then need to develop your business building skills…

Learning Points From Chapter Nine:

1.   Do you regularly contact different people in your downline? How accessible are you?

2.   Do you monitor your network now? Do you know when you need to 'fix it'?

3.   When dealing with new recruits, do you explain the need for purchasing literature to promote the company and the products?

4.   Do you make sure the new recruit actually purchases the required literature and that it's used effectively?

5.   Do you have a system in place to train the new recruit in stages about the marketing plan and the various avenues of income that can be derived from the plan?

Notes:

_____

_____

_____

_____

Chapter Ten

Developing Your Business

Once you have your controls in place and you are able to monitor the activity, you then need to give the network a method of operation, or a way for them to develop their business so that they can make a positive contribution to the ongoing success of the network.

This really relates to Time Management, and this topic warrants an entire book, but we are highlighting here the need to inform your network of the role they will be playing and the fact that your time is precious, so make the best use of it.

Earlier in this book we covered certain aspects of Time Management, especially useful for a relatively new agent or distributor, but here we shall be looking at managing your time from a slightly different perspective.

Eight days a week

In the early months and years you are quite likely to be in full-time employment elsewhere and so it's important that you plan your time carefully to obtain the greatest benefit from your membership with your selected company. As mentioned earlier, great success can be achieved by 'telling everyone you meet what you do' and correct management of your time during this process will greatly assist in the results achievable.

In order to ensure you are making the *best* use of your time at the moment, firstly we need to establish where you currently spend your time and how effective the time is that you spend. Did you complete the 'Questionnaire' in Chapter Six? If so then you will already have a head start on the other people who are reading this chapter first, who will now need to take time out to refer back to Chapter Six!! For their benefit, and yours, a brief reminder may be helpful. How do you currently manage your time? *Do you* currently manage your time?

There are a variety of ways people 'manage' their time:

* Badly! Always rushing, never finishing, frequently apologising, disorganised and distressed – everyone else can see it could be done better.
* Poorly – general lack of planning or forethought, good intentions but few time scales ever met – frustration at knowing things should be done better.
* Well – reasonably good at structuring time planning, actually in some control, partly effective, desire to improve things but unsure how.
* Excellently – very good time planning, *no* wasted time, a full complete and satisfying day/week/month, you achieve at least 95% of your target.
* OTT – a time freak! Spends too much time watching time (seconds!) and not enough time on important things, forgets about 'people' and focuses on events, likely to border on being rude, off-hand and unliked by others.

How many of you fit one of the above categories? *All* of you will, we're sure, see a likeness to yourself in at least one of the above examples, and no doubt recognise similarities for other people you know.

So how can getting 'control' of your time lead to greater control of your income, your prospects and ultimately, your life!? Well, listen very carefully for we shall share some of the secrets with you, and if you want to learn more you will need to attend one of our courses specifically covering this very subject.

The first step to achieving success in the time management process is to firstly, get a calendar/diary/Filofax and clearly write in each week, your family and personal time; next it should be your 'full-time' work time, your social time, leisure time, etc. How much time is left? This is likely to be the time you have available for promoting your company's products or services. As this may not equate to a lot of time in a week/month this time needs to be precision planned for maximum benefit.

In order to gauge the success of the organisation, you need a plan that outlines the steps that you will take in order to achieve success. With an appropriate plan in place, you will then be able to monitor where you are in the overall scheme of things. We spoke about the Wholesale Volume Profit in the last chapter as the means to determine how successful the organisation is, and its growth potential. If you don't have the stages of success highlighted, you will not be able to work your gauges properly because you don't know where you should be.

Ideally, a monthly calendar that is approximately an A4 sheet with a box for each day should be copied and sent to everyone in your organisation. Quarterly is an ideal period in which to outline to the organisation what the sales targets are, what the sales were for the previous quarter, where the organisation is in relation to reaching the goals, and outline all company sponsored events and any meetings you have set for your organisation.

When creating the calendar, it is necessary for you to work the calendar to what you need and want, otherwise the calendar will take advantage of you, and you will be governed by the needs of others.

How much money do you need/want to earn? How many products do you need to sell to achieve this? How many people do you need to talk/meet to achieve this? How are you going to contact (or get into contact with) this number of people?

You need to know the answers to these and other questions. It may not be an easy task to accomplish your targets/goals… or is it?

As mentioned earlier if *you* did all the retailing there may be insufficient time in the day/week to achieve the figures you require. So why not focus a certain amount of your scheduled time to recruit others and get them to retail the products where *you* will receive some of the 'rebate' commission?

You may have realised that the subject of Time Management does not vary too much in its basic principles, that of 'taking control, discipline, initiative, planning and organisation'! By maintaining an effective diary system and paying attention to both clear communication and strong organisation (planning) you can set your sights on many things in life. But now we're slipping back into the need for having an 'objective' – although there is clearly a place for Time Management within this also.

As stated earlier within this book, you need to 'know where you are going' and by taking charge of your available time you can greatly assist yourself in achieving the things which you want and need.

We also discussed earlier the importance of recruiting and we make no apology for re-stating here that it should form part of your overall strategy to recruit a specific amount of people per week/month. There is no definitive number involved to guarantee success for you, but what we can say is that we have never met a person who recruited no-one and still achieved the sums they longed for.

Equally, we have never met a person who recruited dozens of people and who never achieved their initial targets. Planning is required and of course, effective management of your time is crucial.

We suggest you schedule regular organisational meetings for your growing network, preferably during the beginning of the third week of the month, which allows time to make up some of any shortfall in this month's target whilst at the same time you/they can begin planning next month. It also provides an opportunity to 'recognise' the distributors who are doing well which will give both them and others in the group some additional motivation to succeed. This is naturally something you need to set time aside for and should form part of your planning activity for the weeks and months ahead.

The targets/figures you and your network should strive to achieve must relate to the 'volume sold' and not the 'profit' (rebate) earned as your rebate % will change/fluctuate. The 'volume' sold should be equal to or greater than the previous month – always!! If you fail to achieve this in one month it should be 'forgotten' and you start the next month with a clean sheet – much as you do even when you have achieved your target.

The reason for this is that too many people have thought they will make up the shortfall 'next month' and in reality this puts further pressure on them needlessly when they need to plan their time and work to a structured schedule; the additional pressure may provide an initial burst of effort but if/when this does not produce the desired results they will feel even more 'down' and 'beaten' than would otherwise have been the case.

We are not suggesting that questions are not asked of the distributor/you as to why the 'target' was not achieved; there may be a very good explanation, but in recognising the problem (whatever it is) you need to move on and make sure the next month sees the desired improvement – obtain commitment (already discussed).

Therefore, we suggest you always work to ensure your time is effectively spent. How do you do this? When should you start? Ideally you should start immediately – *now!*

What you need to consider is where your time is most effectively spent? With the customers promoting/selling the products or recruiting more new distributors or sitting on a seminar?

This may produce a different answer from each of you, and that's fine, but each of you is different with different requirements from both this business and from your life. You need to know what these are… and manage your time to set a programme in place to achieve them.

Part of the skill in correctly managing your time with your network is to ensure you can effectively devote the 'right' amount of time to each key person and to 'manage' the time spent. Firstly you need to identify these key people. Do you know who the 'key' people are within your growing network? Possibly not, so ensure you read the section within the next chapter which relates to 'The 80/20 Rule'. Basically, you need to know that there are some distributors who deserve your time, and others that take advantage of your time.

It is conceivable that the high producers, with the correct guidance and management, could achieve even greater heights with your assistance and careful planning. Just relay much of what you have learned from this book – you could even buy them a copy today! Once they see for themselves what you have learned, practised and ultimately developed into a successful business, they will want to duplicate it. If it works for you it can work for them too – "How hard can it be?" And with this success it will inevitably bring the business levels up for others within the network as the information is cascaded down throughout and they can see how simple it is to achieve good results.

When you are monitoring the network, you are aware of the activity, you know who is working, and who is not. Those that do not work, determine why and how you can assist them. Those who are working, make sure that they are 'on track' and the pace is right for them.

When you hold your regular network meetings, encourage the network to find new ways to promote their business that they are comfortable with. It is important that the network is capable of working to these ideas, and that they are within the guidelines of the company. Sometimes, what you are comfortable doing others will not be.

Encourage the network to communicate with each other, and maybe do joint shows, hold joint meetings – generally work together. When this happens, your time will be freer.

How do you develop your own personal business further? As you become more confident in your ability to promote the business opportunity and products, others will see this in you and want to join. They will certainly want to join a network that is successful, positive and professional.

To summarise then:

- ❖ Identify where you currently spend your time – what are you doing and when?
- ❖ If you have not done so already, complete the Questionnaire in Chapter Six to assist you
- ❖ Schedule into your diary other events – full-time work, social, family, etc.
- ❖ Identify your 'free time' – to devote to your business development
- ❖ Structure your time – personal sales, recruiting, managing, etc.
- ❖ Identify your 'key' people – work with them to further improve their success
- ❖ Hold regular organisational meetings – for further planning and recognition
- ❖ Having identified the lower producers – separate the 'casual' from the committed
- ❖ Develop a 'track' for your distributors to run on – time and target based
- ❖ Conduct regular reviews of your planning and update if required

We will just add that you should always be honest when analysing where you spend your time as you will identify many areas which can be developed for improving personal sales, recruitment, etc., and also where you can devote more time to your family or social life as well. Imagine how your family would feel if you could regularly spend more 'quality' time with them! And we do mean *quality time*. Not just a couple of minutes sat in front of the television or talking to the neighbours whilst the family remain in the background somewhere.

We mean *real* time with them.

This could include talking to them, playing with them, laughing with them, going out with them, sitting indoors with them, whatever it takes, but *real quality time*. This is easier said than done, but with correct management of your time you can achieve gradual improvements, like with your business, and eventually you will discover a tremendous sense of wellbeing and satisfaction from the results attained.

Managing your time effectively will also assist in other areas of your personal life and business life. This is especially important when considering relaxation and reducing stress – ah! but that's for another book, another course, another time!

Whether you have recently started in Direct Sales or an MLM company, have a small network or an extensive one, the first rule for managing your time remains the same. Remember the earlier statement:

"What is the BEST use of my time RIGHT NOW?"

Think carefully about your answer and then work towards achieving it!

Your main goal with your network should be to manage your time to duplicate yourself – you want as many people as you can to move up the ladder of success within the organisation and benefit from the success found in this position.

How do you do it? You need to have them follow the leader…

Learning Points From Chapter Ten:

1.   I understand how to manage my time, and I regularly use some form of diary.

2.   Do you make use of your time with your downline by holding regular training and opportunity meetings?

3.   I have written down what my financial objectives are, and I constantly strive to achieve them on a month to month basis.

4.   Are your downline aware of your objectives, and have you explained how each member can assist you to achieving those objectives?

Notes:

_____

_____

_____

_____

_____

Chapter Eleven

Follow The Leader

The network builder

This chapter is aimed at the 'network builders'. They will already have a network and wish to ensure network retention, whilst developing and expanding their network.

It is hoped that you have read each chapter of the book, and are now looking for something for 'you' – something that will help you to move that much closer to a stronger and more profitable network.

We have taken this chapter and separated it into sections to make it easier for you to work with.

Part One: Working with the Downline

Importance of product usage – by everyone!

The products that your company have made available to you will enable you to be where you want to be in the future, and they are responsible for where you are today, a successful individual who is building a business, and has achieved an element of success.

Your company has an array of products, possibly personal care, home care, nutritional and weight-loss products, and possibly car care. Do you use all of the products? If not, why not? Why do you not use your own products? Generally, the consumption of company products is less costly than the purchase of similar products from shops. Depending upon the discount level you are at, you could find that you have saved a considerable amount of money.

When you joined the company, you were attracted to the products. Yes, there was some element of interest attached to the possible income that could be earned, but doesn't the quality of the products play an important factor? We would say yes. If the products were of a poor quality, would the company still be in business today, and would the commissions that you earn still be as good as they are today? Probably not. Let us ask you, do you have repeat sales? If the product was of a poor quality, would the customers come back for a re-order? Of course they would not; the fact that they do keep coming back is indicative of a good product at a keen price!

It would be reasonable then to say that, since the customers that you have think the products are good, and you at one time were interested in them, you should still be using the products. And do you think that your network of distributors should also be using the products? How many still do and are you aware of those that don't?

How easy is it to answer a customer's question of how the product works/how it tastes/how you use it, if you have never even seen it, except for the picture in your product brochure?

How confident is your customer that the product is any good? An example, would be a car salesman who works for Mercedes. Does he drive a Ford Fiesta? No, he drives a Mercedes, because he and Mercedes believe in the quality of the product. The same reasoning can be said about your product range. If you don't use the product, nor your downline, why should your customers buy from you? It is an interesting fact that if you do not use the products, your enthusiasm decreases.

It is important to understand from the very beginning that you are a product of the product. Your enthusiasm and confidence in what the products can do will be evident to the customers. If you have had good results from the products, tell your customers. If the products have had good results for a customer, tell another customer. This is an ideal way to promote the other products that your company offers whilst at the same time ensuring you retain and enhance your customer relations.

Your customers want to know that the products will work for them. If you can relate their needs to other customers or distributors who are using the products then you will find that your sales will increase. By your own use of the products, you will be able to relate the stories from customer to customer, and distributor to distributor by adding your own 'testimonial'.

We have been writing here about you using the products to show confidence in the products to your customers. It is also important to show the same confidence to your downline in the products you use. If you are seen to not use them, and you are 'ticking over an income', do you think they will follow you and do the same? Most definitely. This will result in a decrease in the orders placed by your downline.

People need to have a role model, somewhere or something that they can use as the foundation for where they will go. If you don't set the foundation stones, they will have no direction, and probably become one of the vast number who open the door, look inside rather than step inside, and decide to pass the full potential of the opportunity over.

You need to develop a 'Testimonial Book', in the form of a Presentation Book, and we have referred to this concept throughout *Now It's YOUR Turn For Success!* If you truly want it to be your turn… it is important to put your Book together, for yourself, your downline, and your customers.

When you are using the products, you have seen results. If you were on the weight-loss programme, tell people what your results were. Most probably they know you, and have watched your results. But for those who do not know you, you can tell them what happened to you, but it is better to show them what happened to you, and tell them that they too can achieve results from the products. Remember the drama!

Your downline when they first join may not have stories to put in their Book, they will need to borrow your stories, until they have some of their own.

It is important to make the stories/results known to all of your group, so that there is a ready library of stories to choose from. Results from products will vary person to person, and you need to make available a variety of stories with varying degrees of results.

You need to remember that all people are different, and the reasons why they join the company are different. Would it be right to say that your downline is made up of different types of people, some like yourself, some you would like to be like, and possibly one or two that you wouldn't like to be like? But the common factor that holds you all together is the fact that everyone is taking or using the products!

What you need to do when you finish reading this chapter is talk to your downline, and make sure that they understand why they need to start becoming a product of the product. Make sure that they place those orders, and use the products. If they start to shy off, remind them of the generous discount they will enjoy! An added bonus to you is that if they start to place more orders for personal use products, your commission cheques will go up!

Tell, Show, Try, Do – all aspects of the business

How do you work with your downline now? Do you blind them with knowledge in one hit, expect them to remember all of it, then move to the next one when your expectations are not met? Do you think that this is a practical approach?

In order to build a network, you need to work one step at a time, and at the pace of the recruit, not yours. This is vital to the longevity and output of the recruit.

Tell the recruit what they need to do. Let's say for example you are going to help them recruit a few distributors. They want to progress through the various commission levels the way you have. So, what do you do? You can give them an outline of a pre-sentation for recruiting, let them read it, make sure they understand the reasons why things are done in a certain way. Then what do you do? Leave them to get on with it? No.

You then *show* them how to do it, following what you have told them. Ideally, you would help them with their own list of people that they want to share the opportunity with. Actually pick up the phone, call a name on the list, introduce yourself, why you are calling, on behalf of whoever, and that you want to share a business opportunity with them. Sounds good so far? Now what do you do? Leave them to get on with it on their own? No.

You now sit with them and let them *try* to follow what you have just done, and make sure that they are comfortable with what they are doing, that they are following the steps you have laid out.

Make sure that they are improving every time they try. When you are sure that they are competent, then let them *do* it on their own. You don't need to be there hovering over them.

We have just highlighted one aspect, that of recruiting someone from the list. But this system carries through everything that you do as a leader – how to put the Testimonial Book together, how to demonstrate the products, how to conduct an opportunity meeting, retailing the products, even down to how you manage your day.

That is the tell, show, try, do system. It is very effective, and gives the new recruit the independence that they need, and you also, because you need to go on to the next new recruit, and do the same thing all over again!

The '72 Hour' Rule

What does this mean? Do you have a distributor that you have signed up, and weeks have gone by and nothing has happened? No calls back to you, no orders, not even for personal use, and no recruits? Everyone must have at least one such distributor. There could be quite a number of reasonable explanations for this situation, but it is highly likely that because the 72 Hour Rule did not take place, nothing will become of this recruit. Basically, their enthusiasm for either the product, the company or the concept has waned.

Let us ask another question. How many of you had signed your application form, and immediately ordered product? How many ordered product the next day? How many the day after that? You will be pleased to know that you formed part of the 72 Hour Rule. Do you have any idea yet what this means? Someone who gets involved in your business, and orders product immediately, is more likely to continue with the company than someone who signs in and then sits back and waits for something to happen. Most of you are proof that this rule is valid. You got involved and very quickly placed your first orders.

What impact did your sponsor have in placing this first order very quickly? If they were doing their job effectively, chances are they were aware of the 72 Hour Rule, and were merely building their business, and you have become a part of that.

You need the enthusiasm of the initial product order followed immediately by the retail sale to create momentum for the individual to carry on. There are three types of people in this world:

1. Those people who **MAKE** things happen
2. People who **WATCH** things happen
3. People who **WONDER** what happened

There are quite a number of people out there who are quite happy to sit and watch life pass them by; each one of you can think of at least one person you have recently been in contact with who is a 'watcher'. They happily 'watch' what to do and how to do it, but effectively do nothing themselves. They just sit and watch! What you as a distributor need to ensure is that you do not recruit too many 'watchers' into your business. The result will be a failed business because they are all waiting for something to happen!

There are others who sit and 'wonder' what happened. They wonder how others are successful, and just how did you get to be so successful – we wonder!

What you need are 'doers' – those people who see the opportunity that you are presenting to them, and who immediately act to share the information with others, regardless of whether or not it is a product sale or a new recruit.

It is amazing to observe people. If you set the example, people follow. If there is no example, very rapidly a group of people with no direction, no idea of what should or should not be done, and to what particular order, will fall apart before your eyes.

Have you ever experienced a series of distributors drop off one after the other from your network? It is probable that there was no direction from their immediate upline and as a result, they left.

Remember the phrase used in an earlier chapter "If you don't know where you're going, how are you going to know when you get there?" This relates exactly to not only you, but also your complete downline.

Ensure they have a clear *direction!*

The 'doers' that you are looking for need the instant activity because that starts to create the urgency to accomplish something. If the commitment to do something is there from the distributor, they stand a very good chance of following through with their plan.

In summary, you need to ensure that the new recruits you meet order the product immediately, if not for themselves, for a customer they have. This enthusiasm and sense of achievement at the beginning will often help them to create the momentum they need to continue.

Both you and they need a clear direction, something to focus on and believe in, something which is achievable and desirable. Go for it!

Developing goals and plan of action – by everyone!

You cannot achieve your goals if you don't know what they are!

How many people reading this book know what they are going to be doing for the rest of the day? How many people know what they will be doing this week? How many people have a fairly good idea of how the next week will shape? How many have no idea, and are going to sit back and watch to see what happens?

For those of you who know what you are planning to do this week, have you got the details written down, or are you so sure of what you want to achieve you can visualise what needs to happen?

What about your downline? Do you know their goals, what their plan of action is? How will you know what help, support and encouragement you need to give to your network if you have no idea why they are in the business? Again, the phrase above applies, "If you don't know where you're going, how are you going to know when you get there?" Work with them at their own level of commitment, don't push your ideas/concepts on them.

This is a very basic step in leadership that many people will overlook, and the reason why is that the person doing the 'leading' has no goals set down. There is no plan in place, no clear idea of what they want from the company.

The first thing that you need to do is set your own goals. Where do you want to be next month? Do you want to see yourself at the next extravaganza? Do you want your name and photograph published in the company promotional literature? Do you know what you need to do to get there? How will you get there? Do you plan to do it yourself, or will you enlist the help of your network? With a plan involving your network, you need to take control and lead the group to accomplish what you set out to achieve. Along the way, the network will start to accomplish what they also set out to achieve. Everybody can win!

You need to tell your group what it is that you want to achieve, and what part they are going to play in the success. If you put ideas or plans in print, there is a better chance that the plans will happen. Take your plans, put them in print, and let your network know what part they will contribute in the plan. Make sure that your distributors know how you are progressing with your plans. For example, if your goal is to attend the next company international convention, you will need a certain amount of sales volume created by you and your network.

You must first develop a plan whereby you know what the monthly target will be. This should, over the period of qualification for the trip, see you achieve your goal. It is important to let those around you who are participating in your success know how successful they are in assisting you in achieving your goals.

When you are seeking the assistance of your network, and you are keeping them informed of your progress, a strange thing will start to happen – your network of distributors will start to achieve their goals, and increase their sales – which will result in your goals being realised!

By knowing what the goals are of your distributors, what it is that they want to accomplish, as a result of promoting the company products, you can tie this in with your plan.

You then are in a position to take control of your network, you are better able to steer the group to the success you want to achieve. If you help your network to meet their goals, say for example attaining a certain level that will increase their bonus, your group volume will increase, thus increasing your overall income derived from the network.

How will you get your organisation to set their own plans of action? It may be a bit difficult to go back to each and every one of your distributors after reading this book and tell them you want their plan of action, what they want to achieve in the immediate future, what their long term plans are, and when they want to achieve all of this by – just so that you can help them! This would be, in most cases, extremely difficult to achieve if for no other reason than dealing with the practicalities of the distances involved between you and your network.

However, you can go to those you are in close contact with, both geographically and personally, those individuals that you know work with their own little groups, and have them relay the information.

Ideally, from today, each and every person you sponsor should be asked to write down their goals, and you work with them to create a plan of action of how the company can help them to achieve their goals. Very simply, if they want to earn only £100 per month, show them what products they need to sell to achieve that level of commission.

If they want to recruit in addition to retailing the product, show them how many people they need to sponsor each month, and what volume of business they need to be generating. When you are doing your follow-up with them, remind them of what you helped them to put in place, and why. There may be a need to contact this person to remind them of their action plan if their sales/recruiting is dropping off.

Building wide and deep

What do we mean by this statement? "How wide is too wide?" "How deep is deep?" For several reasons you are about to discover, it is a good idea to work below the level of cut-off for your commission.

Ideally, if you are reading this book with thoughts of joining a company in the near future, you need to ensure that the company you are looking at has depth, and preferably will pay a bonus on at least three to five levels. If, however, you are already well established within a company, you might need to refer to their marketing plan (or equivalent) booklet to discover how many levels they pay out too. Hopefully it will be between at least three to five levels. The bonus or 'payout' should be at least 4%. Some plans will pay less, but then the payment will come from a deeper pay out line. In MLM you need the numbers – the new recruits, as this will help to take up the slack for those recruits who may not work to either your expectations or theirs.

There is a well known phrase;

"The day you stop recruiting is the day you start to fail"

This is one of the most important things that you need to remember when you are building your MLM business. You must never stop recruiting and become complacent about the size of your organisation. Anything can happen to change the structure, and some of the changes that will take place will be out of your control. But, for those things that you have control over, continue to recruit. The result of continual recruiting will help to compensate for the periods when you have distributors who will not order, or decide to leave. In order to keep your organisation thriving, you need to continually recruit new blood.

To give you an example of what can happen below the level that you are paid, I can relate an incident which happened to me (Janet) several years ago and which served as a useful experience.

I had personally sponsored a young girl, who recruited her friend, a hairdresser, who recruited another friend, and so on, down about seven levels. All of these people were promoting the business part-time, and were looking for a short-term way of earning extra cash. However, there was someone further down in the network who was currently involved in an MLM organisation, and for various reasons, the business was not sufficiently 'exciting'.

All of the part-time people eventually went their various ways, but this one person, through persistence, found who had sponsored whom, all the way back to me. I was duly contacted, and the discussion was very successful – this individual became full-time, and eventually contributed to a substantial percentage of my income.

So what did I learn? I learned a very good lesson from this experience – after that, *every* piece of paper, every product, every distributor kit that went out of my door had *my name, address and phone number attached to it!* I knew I was lucky to catch this one, but didn't want to run the risk of losing any others!

Continual recruiting and asking 'Who do you know?' will not in itself build your organisation. As leaders, you must build your organisation.

Recruiting is not just checking if the person has a pulse, and if it is there, sponsor them. We have all had our share of those people, and later in this chapter we will go into a bit more depth on 'quality' recruiting.

What you need to understand very early on is that you need to be working with your organisation below the level of pay out, and to build as wide an organisation as you can as an insurance because, one day, you may get paid on those people. When you work below the pay line, you create depth, and depth will create security – security in continuing to create growth of your organisation. If anyone in your organisation should drop out, you have secured a replacement further down in the network that will roll up to you, thus ensuring the continuity of payment.

Let us give you an example of a key person from another well known internationally successful company with offices in England, and share with you what happened to him.

A very good friend of ours in England is a highly successful MLMer, and over the last fourteen years has now earned over £1 million from one company. He has over the years recruited and built a worldwide organisation. One of his distributors in England recruited someone in another European country, who quickly sponsored over one-hundred people in his own country. The group started to disintegrate very quickly because of a lack of follow-through, but one person who stayed on started to sponsor.

This person was out of our friend's payline, but as our friend worked his entire organisation, when the roll-up happened, there were no surprises, for our friend knew exactly what each person was aiming for, and finally our friend got paid on his efforts. How much? Over three consecutive months this fellow earned enough money to purchase a substantial family home in the South of England, just from this group alone. Does this sound like the sort of concept you need to adopt in your business plan? We would think so!

Part Two: The Importance of Promotion

Promoting company events

Everyone should write this phrase down and remember it:

"If you promote, you go to the bank."

Do you understand what this phrase means? What it means quite simply is the need to take full advantage of events that the company promote.

It is important to note that the company meeting itself is not so important, it will take place with or without you, but how you promote the event is important.

An average meeting with above average promotion will result in *great* success.

Think about the last company event you went to. Before you went, what were you told to expect? Were you told that it was a day was for key leaders? Were you told to ensure all your distributors attended? Was it a day you were not to miss? Also, you might have been told that there would be elements of the day that would help you promote your business, ultimately leading you to even greater success!

Just as the company did a great job promoting their event, you as key leaders need to learn to promote the company events. You need to understand that these events are not put in place because the management staff need something to do one weekend. You need to understand that these events are put in place in order for you to take full advantage of what the company represents, both in terms of products available, and the compensation plan that is available to you for the successful promotion of these products. You need to understand how the compensation plan works – in other words, what you need to do in order to generate a good standard of living, either full-time or part-time.

You should also remember that the events will take place whether you are there or not. Let us ask you, would you rather sponsor a person, tell them a bit about the company, then let them talk to someone in the hope of sponsoring them, but understanding that your new recruit doesn't yet fully understand the marketing plan, and have them in turn speak to someone else? Is there a possibility that the fifth person's version of the compensation plan would be totally different from the one that you have come to understand?

If the compensation plan gets distorted, it is possible other bits of information will also be distorted. Let's say you find out about this situation, and you then have to spend your valuable time unravelling this mess. Is this time well spent? There is a possibility that it will not be the best way to be building your business.

Let's now say you are actively recruiting people, because you have your plan of action written out, and you know how many new recruits you need to create a certain amount of volume that will help you to achieve your goals. You are going to be very busy this next quarter, as you need to sponsor let's say twenty people. There is going to be a certain amount of time spent seeing these people, giving them the basic training to get them started, get them started on the products, follow up to make certain that they are in fact using the products properly. You may need to spend of bit of time with them understanding the first few steps of the marketing plan. Do you agree that some time needs to be spent with these people? Yes!

You are going to be a busy person because, added to your business opportunity, you have a full-time job, and three children at home, and you are having your sister and her family of four children planning to come and stay next month. Can you relate to this situation? You are not alone, this situation is quite common, and sometimes even more hectic! So, take this situation we have just highlighted, and you are going to recruit and train twenty new people.

What are you going to do? To start with, we suggest you take advantage of the company events and bring your people along. If there is local training, or at least at a location close to you, and you cannot attend, that does not stop your group from attending. Any information you obtain for meetings, rallies, training days, etc. copy the information and send it to your organisation. What better way to be trained/hear new information/talk to others than to attend company events where the individuals get the information first hand!

These events are there to be used by you, so you need to take full advantage of what is offered to you. If you attend a company event this month on your own, and you know it will be run again next quarter, do you want to attend again, and bring along some of your key distributors? Would you like them to bring people along? We would think you might!

You may be working to a tight budget/don't like where you live/don't have a good means of transportation. But, you need to make the effort to attend the company events, and ensure that you continue to have as many people from your organisation attend, and they in turn invite their new recruits. Maximise the benefits available to all concerned.

The company event will be put together very professionally, and at a cost greater than you could probably have afforded or wanted to pay for, and the distributor can also meet other people just like themselves who have chosen the company as a means to achieve their success.

As well as promoting and selling the products, you need to sell the *drama* of the company event. Not just, there will be another training Saturday again, do you want to attend? But rather with enthusiasm about who will be there and what they will be doing. You have no idea who will be doing the training on Saturday, they build a business... they have achieved... you just cannot miss hearing what they have to say! You may have heard that person so many times that if you hear them again you may scream, but to that new person, it's the very first time; they are new, encourage their enthusiasm. Do you agree that it is better use of your time to have twenty people at the same time attend a company training day?

When there has been a series of events, you need to say how great the last one was, it was unbelievable, but this next one will be even better still because… Ensure that they do not want to miss the event. Create the 'vision', the excitement, the drama, the "I am not going to miss this one". You must have the right attitude, and belief in what you can and will do.

Promoting yourself – the need for a story

"Facts will Tell… Stories will Sell"

You know how well you have done, and you probably have a good idea of how well you will do in the future. Quite possibly some of your network know this also, but what about the person who does not know you yet? Is your personal success either on the products or with the business known to this person? No, it is not. Telling is one thing, but showing is even better. Do you remember this phrase, 'A picture is worth a thousand words'? If you have had results on the weight-loss programme, have a before and after picture. If your achievements in the company have been outstanding, what proof have you got? Do people want to know? Yes, they do. These people are ordinary people like you and they just want some reassurance that the decision they made is the right one. You can help them.

Remember earlier we wrote about the Testimonial Book? Well, you need to bring it out again and add to it. Put in some proof of what the products can do. If they are not your stories, then use the stories of your downline. But you need to remember that other people's stories have no value unless your story is added. They are abstract, no life.

People that you are going to speak to about the opportunity and the products will want to know about you. Not thirty minutes of "I thought about the opportunity, the following week I found my first distributor… six months later I did…" If they haven't fallen asleep by this point, they will think the business is too slow for them!

You need to develop a very short one minute story on yourself – hit them with intensity, add the now legendary *drama* to the story, make sure that it is punchy, and will get people's attention. You need to add the drama to give the story life. Then you need to practise saying it over and over again, with feeling, so that it does not sound like you have memorised it or that it is just a script you are reading!

You could say, "I lost eight pounds on the products in two weeks. I felt terrific and told my friends and family, and now one year on I have my own business and I turn over xx per month, and you could too!" You can take any of the products that you have had success with and alter this message. If we said this to you, would you think about the opportunity? We would think most of you reading this book would, especially if you were looking for an opportunity to earn some extra money. Remember, if you don't need to say it, leave it out.

It is important to take into consideration how other people perceive your business. You may be able to talk about it for hours, and you are really excited about your progress, and you fall into the trap of telling a prospect *everything* in the space of several hours.

The prospect may take the view that what they had just witnessed was a standard sales presentation to the business opportunity. This may result in them declining the offer, no matter how tempting it sounded because they knew that they did not have the available time to spend on the business. People's perception of how the business works is based on how you bring them in to it. People don't want you to sit and talk to them for two or three hours. After this time the prospect will give you the excuse that they don't have the time to spend promoting the business that you have. If you give them a short, sharp presentation, they are more likely to listen to you, and follow what you do when they become one of your distributors.

As time goes on, you need to highlight your progression with the company. Those people that are going to be a part of your network in the future need to know that they are dealing with a serious and committed person! Right? If you are planning to make it to the top, there are going to be some people that you will need to take along with you, and these people need to know how serious you are! They will also need to have a plan so that they can follow you and contribute to your success, and theirs as well!

You can demonstrate to these key people that by promoting the products that the company has to offer you are able to earn a certain amount of money. If the products were not of a high quality, if you were not committed to the company, then you would not have achieved the level of income you are currently enjoying.

There is a time and a place when you need to demonstrate to people just how well you are doing, and that they can also enjoy the same results, or possibly earn more than you. The existing distributors that you have, and those that you will continue to recruit, should be aware that the earning potential is unlimited. You want recruits who don't want a ceiling on their earnings potential, who have the vision to go further than you.

Those distributors who are currently in your network need to be encouraged to surpass you, for if they surpass you, you will still earn from them, as long as you are meeting the company targets for payment.

This is one of the benefits of the 'Breakaway' plan; those below you can exceed you, and you can still be paid!

As you gain experience and distributors, expand your story to five minutes and ten minutes, and use these stories when the time is appropriate, but remember to keep the *drama* evident! Once you have your story, you then need to promote your network.

Promoting your network

It follows on that not only is your story important, but the stories of your network are important. You need to do more than just create your own stories, you need to teach this to your networks. Make sure each one has a product story and a progression story.

Remember we said earlier if you needed to, borrow stories from your downline?

This is important because you will not be able to cover all of the 'testimonials' for all of the products, but it is highly likely that some of your distributors can. Not only mention their product success, but their customer success. You will also need to highlight their business success. Why? The prospective distributor sitting in front of you needs to know they are making the right decision. Not only are you successful, but in your Testimonial Book you can show them other people who have found varying degrees of success.

Make sure that you put a story in about someone who only does this business part-time, yet is able to create xx number of volume points per month. Highlight someone who is a dedicated retailer. Someone again who does a combination of retailing and recruiting. Cover yourself from the low to the high, culminating with your own story. You can say, "Because of people like this in my organisation, I am able to enjoy xx, and you can too!"

Teaching the art of promotion

This will be a summary of what we have just been reading about. The enthusiasm of the events to come, combined with how great past events/people have been, creates the *drama* necessary to sustain the momentum to create an explosive organisation.

You need to have a sense of urgency about building your business. You want to be successful, and you want it now! You need to enlist the help of those you have recruited to get you there. That is why you recruit the type of person we spoke about earlier, the 'doers' who will make things happen, not only for themselves, but for you also. There has never been an MLM business built by 'watchers'!

Take what the company promotes, and use it. Use the brochures the company spend time and money producing. Make the effort to bring/invite people to the training seminars the company provides. Most importantly, make the effort to use the products the company supply, and talk to people about them, and what they can do for *them!*

If you do not tell people what you do, they cannot read your mind. Do not prejudge anyone by thinking they would not be interested in the business/products. They may not be interested, but they may know someone who would be interested.

The company offers professionally designed literature, use it. The company supplies you with high quality products, use them. The company offers an excellent compensation plan, follow it and show others how to achieve high results. The company puts seminars/training days together for you, use them.

If you are promoting your own events, you need to know that if you put above average promotion into an average meeting, it will result in great success. You will remember that we said this earlier on, but you need to know that average will still give you success. You may view your own organisational meetings as average, based on how you feel about your own ability. Don't worry, average will still give results – but just imagine what above average could produce!

Never before has such an opportunity been available to you than the one which presents itself to you now. The opportunity to become involved in other people's success and know that you have contributed significantly.

Aside from great satisfaction and pleasure, the real benefit to you is that you will also be achieving your own success!! So recruit quality...

Part Three: Quality Recruitment

The three stages of a recruit

Are all recruits alike? Can you predict what your recruits are going to do?

What kind of recruits do you most like to deal with? Why do you like dealing with this type of recruit? Quite often you can relate the three stages of a recruit to that of a child, a teenager and an adult. Let us explain.

Has it ever happened to you that you have a new recruit, and they do well, just like a child, they listen to what you have to say, they do what you say and everything is going along just fine, and then one day, that recruit doesn't do what you have told him/her to do anymore. They misbehave, don't do as you advise, they do their own thing and rebel?

Do you sit back and wonder what happened? Has this happened to you more than once? This is generally quite normal, your recruit has just moved to the next stage of being a recruit, a typical teenager.

It is important when you are building your organisation that you build wide and deep – we covered this earlier in the chapter. When we have finished this section on the three stages of a recruit, you may understand better why you should be continually recruiting.

New recruits are fun to have. They give you a boost, you see their enthusiasm and eagerness to get as much information as they can from you. Because of their enthusiasm, you find yourself enthusiastic, and everything is running smoothly. You teach and train this new person and give them every piece of information you can to help them build their business. They get results, and they come back to you for more. Life is great, and your income has increased while all this is going on. Have we all been here? Did we all enjoy this time?

Some of you may have been fortunate enough to have two or three new recruits, or more, all going through this phase, and that is fantastic!

Then what happens? One day the new recruit questions what you have said! They even go further and produce their own 'professional' material, and they have decided what to put in this material! You know it's not right, and try as hard as you can, this recruit does not listen. You may find the recruit speaks up and tells you that because they have been in the business four months, and done xx sales, they have now 'peaked' and reached the top rung of the ladder of knowledge. They don't need you, you don't do the business right, and besides, they know all there is to know.

Now, you as the sponsor have been in the business five years, or more, go to all the sponsored company events, read up on the industry, learn about your products, attend seminars to help you deal with people, etc., and this person has just told you they now know more than you! What do you do?

Does this sound like a recruit you have in your organisation?

Do you know what has happened to this wonderful recruit?

If you have children, do you have a teenager? And if so, do you have a rebellious teenager? What do you do with that teenager? Do you enjoy having them around? How are they with the younger children? Do you feel that they are a good influence? When you go out, are you relieved when they don't want to come with you?

In case you haven't worked this one out, you now have a rebellious teenager at home, and you may have two or three in your network. There is no getting away from them!

So, what will you do? What you do is absolutely nothing. Those of you with teenagers can talk to those people without teenagers and tell them the horror stories of being the parent of a teenager.

Like a teenager, the more you try, the farther the distributor will pull away from you. This would be the common response and approach that most people would follow. Persistence of trying to enforce your thinking on the individual to change their attitude will be the approach many will incorrectly follow. Others will save their strength and valuable time, avoid any confrontation and find more of those nice 'new' recruits who will listen to you, those that make you feel good, ultimately ignoring the 'teenager'.

In fact, the route that should be taken would be to leave the teenager alone to get on with their business. Not to ignore them, but not to be overly attentive either. Stand by in the wings ready to help if you are asked. Don't push them, but maybe keep in touch by post, send them details of forthcoming events in the company. Keep in touch, *but at a distance.* This is a wait-and-see time and is the best way to handle this type of recruit.

If you wait and see, there is the possibility that the 'teenager' will change.

Again, if you had a teenager that was rebellious, did he or she one day wake up and remember you were the parent and start to behave differently towards you? Your teenager has started to mature into an adult!

This is a time of relief for the parents, because you had this nightmare that your son or daughter was going to spend the rest of their life looking and acting like some strange person you didn't want to know. All of a sudden the 'young adult' starts to ask you for help and guidance, they offer to do things for you. They appear almost like before, but more mature.

You are relieved! Life is worth carrying on again. You have someone that will listen to you, and you are able to share ideas with them.

Just as your children grow and become teenagers, then mature into young adults, your distributor will also. Your new recruit is just like a baby or a small child. Eager to please, will listen to you, and be guided by what you say and do. They will mimic you. No questioning of what you say or do ever happens. Then quite suddenly they think they know everything, and rebel. All you can do is let them get over this phase, but keep in touch from a distance. You need to wait and see if they come out of this phase. If they do, it is as a 'young adult' and they are keen again to learn.

An example that everyone can relate to of this 'young adult' phase. Imagine a distributor who has rebelled, then suddenly starts to order product again, you see that they have resumed their recruiting, and suddenly you see them at a local distributor meeting. You very casually try to see what paperwork they have with them, remembering their 'phase' or you try to listen to what they are saying. You are surprised to hear that this person is once again following the guidelines as set out by the company. This distributor has come full circle, and will once again be a valuable member of your organisation.

You can have some personal satisfaction in the knowledge that what they have put you through, they will at some time in the future experience themselves!

There is an important phrase to remember about the recruits that you will be recruiting:

"Don't be afraid to let them fail – that is their choice."

What is the solution to this dilemma? – recruit more potential recruits.

It is important for you to be aware that there are people out there who want to be successful in MLM, but for reasons that you have no control over, or reasons that you will never know about, some people will fail. Don't worry, just recruit more people. For every distributor that will fail, there will be several that will not, and they will achieve some element of success.

The need to consistently build your organisation not only in width but depth will help you to have fresh, new distributors continually joining, ordering product, retailing the products, and recruiting, and hopefully cover for the periods when your 'teenagers' are most inactive!

So much to do, so little time – so plan it!

Do you feel that there is never enough time in the day to deal with all the needs of your organisation? Probably quite a number of readers! Do you have distributors call you, and you are unable to get back to them for maybe one or two days?

Life is hectic, isn't it?

You have your full-time family commitments, you may have some work commitments for a job that you do where you are paid a salary, and you are trying to build a successful organisation, retail your products, and try at the end of the day to give yourself maybe half an hour of time to yourself.

You have targets set by the company for promotional events, extra bonuses for production and recruiting, and you want to achieve them. Most important, each and every one of you may have some aspirations to become the top distributor in the company! From experience, we can tell you that you need to stop and evaluate what you are doing first.

But how do you stop the treadmill that you have found yourself on? We have covered 'Time Management' in an earlier chapter, but briefly, you firstly need to take the time to write down how you spend your day. What do you do during the day that is important? Then, systematically go through and see what you can do to work smarter, not harder.

When you are aware of how you spend your day or week, you need to assess what has priority. Take a calendar for the week, and first of all, mark out the time you spend with your family. This will include mealtimes, family time maybe when your children come home from school, when you may help them with their homework, or read to them. This is important, mark it off your calendar.

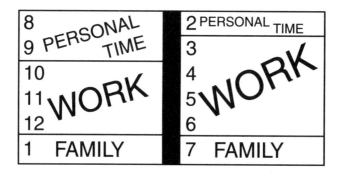

Next you have to assess what time you need for yourself. You need your own time, which could be for studying, prayer time, getting your hair done, or maybe you go and exercise, mark this off on your calendar too.

Do you have other work commitments? If you do, then mark this off also.

What time have you got left? Doesn't look like you have as much time left as you might have thought, and as this is the precious network building time, you need to take full advantage of it.

The '80/20' rule

Let's examine your existing network. Do you try to speak to everyone in your organisation? Are there some people that you speak to more than others? Yes, then let's concentrate on these people for a moment. Why do you speak to each and every one? What *value* do you get from these conversations? You must at this point in the development of your organisation start to understand that not everyone will deserve your undivided attention. They may feel they are entitled to your time, any time they need you, but reality is this small section of time that you have left to build your business.

Have you ever heard of the 80/20 rule? Statistically speaking, 20% of your organisation will do 80% of your business! Or, to put it another way, 80% of your organisation will only do 20% of your business. In this 80% there will also be those distributors who never attend a company sponsored event, they never attend any of your organisation meetings, but occasionally they will order a bit of product, and recruit an occasional distributor. You find that when you keep calling it is more frustrating each time, because nothing happens.

Now you have three categories for your network and from a Time Management perspective:

* The 20% that do 80% of your business – give them your personal time

* The 80% that do 20% of your business – give them your group time

* The 'don't show' – give them mail time

What is your personal time? That is the time that you spend one on one with a person who is getting on with building their business. They don't need you except for stimulation and motivation. They get on with recruiting and retailing, and you need them as much as they need you. The motivation and stimulation runs both ways. You will both benefit from each other. You won't have many of these people, and in the early stages you will spend more time with these people, and as they grow, less and less time, as they become more independent. They are able to duplicate what you do. We will speak about duplication in the next section.

What do we mean by group time? This is the time that you spend at your organisational meetings, the company sponsored meetings, anywhere where a group of your distributors meet. Would everyone agree it is a better use of your time to tell the company story once to twenty people than have to repeat the story twenty times, once to each of the twenty? Bear in mind the precious time we highlighted earlier.

What about the person who calls and asks questions, but doesn't seem to get on with building their own business? Well, you need to learn two words, and we would suggest that you write them down now and place the paper somewhere prominent so that you can refer to it often.

STRATEGY   DIPLOMACY

Firstly, you need to learn *Strategy*. Having a good strategy in business is what you are reading about now. You also need *Diplomacy*. Everyone will have their own level of diplomacy they work to, and the occasions they use this diplomacy will vary from one distributor to another. Sometimes it will be necessary to be extremely diplomatic when dealing with poor performance from members of your downline who are very close to you. Other times the level and extent of your diplomacy will be very little, to ensure you 'get the point across!'

Here is a good example of how to handle someone who constantly asks questions but does nothing, and attends very few events; "That is a good question, John, bring that question to the next meeting and I will answer it so that everyone can benefit from the answer". Not all situations will be that easy, and a few will require much thought, so practise your diplomacy!

Now, something that you need to be aware of with the 80% who should be getting your group time – they want to have your personal time, and unless you learn the 'Art of Diplomacy', you will find that your time will not be as you planned it to be. You must keep remembering that you have only got a few precious hours each day or week in which you build your business, so remember this and plan your time accordingly.

Duplication

"You cannot teach that which you
are not prepared to do yourself"

We have just been focusing on your limited amount of time for your business building, and you have probably realised that you don't have as much time as you thought you had. Do you have any idea what you need to be doing in order to accomplish your goals, or follow your action plan?

You could try and divide yourself in half, and be in two places at once, or share the workload of creating the volume that will in turn give you the bonuses, and generate the income that you want or need. It will probably be easier to share the workload.

Where do you start? We can refer back to the 80/20 rule. The first place to start looking for distributors to share the workload will be in the 20% group, that is the 20% that produce 80% of your business. These people have a desire to succeed and they are already creating a great proportion of your group volume.

You need to assess each of these people. You need to be looking for several things – firstly, do they have a plan of action? If they don't, help them to create one, and ensure that they stick to it.

Secondly, make sure that all the knowledge that you have gained you pass on to them. Not just what you have learned from this book, but any other information that you may have at home. Put a newsletter together that over a period of time forms a small training programme.

And thirdly, share with these people your plan of action, where you want to be in thirty days, ninety days, one year. If you let them know what you are working towards, and that they can play an important role in your success, they will work with you.

Are these distributors like yourself, pressed for time? It will be good if they are, because they see how you are working, and they will follow your actions.

While you are looking inside your organisation, you need to be aware of what to look for when you are recruiting. Do you want anyone who has a pulse to sign the distributor application form? Not really, because you want people to be able to duplicate what you are doing. If they can see the business opportunity that you are offering them, and they judge for themselves what rewards they can obtain, then you want them.

It is important to remember, when you are recruiting, that you want recruits who don't want a ceiling on their earnings potential. In other words, let them decide what they want to earn, not you. Many adverts have been found in newspapers that state 'Earn from X to XXX'. What do you do if someone wants to earn more than that?

Many leaders in the industry will also say to someone about the business opportunity that you can earn from X to XXX with this company when they are doing a presentation.

Ideally, you want those people that you personally sponsor to decide for themselves how much they want to earn. The more that they earn, you have the potential to earn also. So, encourage them as much as you can.

These people are a key to the success and strength of your front line, those people that you have personally sponsored. This level should be the level that creates the width of your organisation. This level of distributor is independent, a duplication of yourself. The more first level distributors that you have in place, the better the insurance that when someone drops out, or slows down, you don't need to worry too much because you have the group volume being created. The success comes from the numbers that are in place.

Note the following example, where you are recruiting five, and each in turn also recruit five:

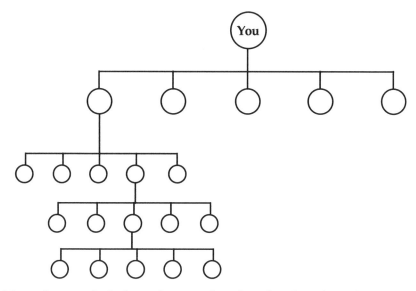

How do you feel about having five first level? What about ten? What about fifty? There is no problem with any of these numbers. Why? It's all in how you plan your organisation. If you are comfortable with dealing with five people, then recruit five first level people. Work with them, show them how the business works, how the products work. Remember the Tell, Show, Try, Do? When you have successfully accomplished this, recruit five more, repeat what you have just done, then go on and recruit five more, and so on.

Should you only work five at a time? There is no right or wrong number of people that you should be recruiting at any one time other than recruiting the number that you are comfortable with. It may not be five, it may be ten or even fifty. Whatever the number, remember the duplication process will kick in. If you recruit and work with five, so will your network. Maybe you could talk yourself into being comfortable recruiting ten at a time?

If you create the excitement in your organisation that you are going places, and that the network can benefit from your success, do you know what? Your network will work with you! Why will they? Quite simply because success has the uncanny ability to be contagious!

When you build your business quickly, and with success, you create momentum and a sense of urgency, and this can make the ride to the top that much easier!

Who you recruit can play a tremendous amount in the success of your business. We know of many people in the Sports and Entertainment industries who are actively and successfully involved in MLM and Direct Sales. There are people involved in this industry who play an active role in the shaping and running of governments around the world. In fact apparently, one of the past Presidents of the United States of America was also an MLMer!! If it's good enough for him...

Wouldn't it be wonderful to recruit a 'personality' into your network? Imagine the impact on your credibility and the associated kudos when you inform potential new recruits that you have someone very famous within your organisation! Think of the centre of influence this 'personality' will have, and all of the people they know, and how they could build their new business enterprise with you... draw up your hit list and start phoning now!

This could be an idea that you want to adopt for your plan of action – you want to recruit someone who is well known into your business.

You may need to elicit the support and assistance from your downline, as one of them may know someone who knows someone...

Commitment

If you decide to go out for the day and say visit a family member in the north, and you have called them, and everything is arranged, they are expecting you, would you suddenly on the journey change your mind and go home? No, you wouldn't, because you have put time into planning the day and who you will visit, you made the phone call, put petrol in the car, and spent several hours driving. Of course you would finish the journey!

You were *committed* to complete the journey.

The same can be said about your business. You invested time and money so far, and you see the business as the vehicle to help you obtain your goals, a new car in your driveway, maybe live in a better area, a better school for your children, or even just the satisfaction of knowing that you have been able to help people get better health, if you have joined a health and nutrition company. Whatever the reasons for joining the company, you made a commitment, and you are following that commitment today by buying and reading a copy of this book to gain more knowledge, develop more skills in the constant pursuit for the success of your business.

Your network that you are building must also have commitment.

What do they want from the company? Ask them when you recruit them what they want from the company. Write down their goals, put them somewhere that they can be seen daily – the bathroom mirror? As the goal is reached, take it off, put up a new one. When the distributor is not positive about the business, remind them of the goals/plan of action they set for themselves.

If the business gets difficult, do you quit? No, you do not, you stick it out, you work harder to make the successes, because you know that it will get better. You have faith in the company to deliver to you products of an excellent quality, and on time!

When you recruit someone new into the business, you want them to commit to a plan of action, based on the time that they have available. Part of that commitment is the purchase of product for personal use.

Remember earlier on we wrote about the 72 Hour Rule? Make sure that it happens. Remember the duplication process; if you recruit someone and they purchase product immediately, as they know nothing any different, they will do the same thing when they are recruiting and use the 72 Hour Rule. The result will be increased group volume.

Commitment is also there from the company you are associated with.

They are committed to deliver to you the best products they feel are available, and they will pay you on time. The company is committed to help you develop, not only within the company, but as an individual.

You show commitment to your customers by ensuring that you organise the delivery of their products, on time. You answer their questions. You show an interest in their welfare. Why should you show so much interest in your customers?

Quite possibly they will become your future distributors!

Remember we mentioned earlier in the book that generally customers make very good distributors. By using the products for a period of time, they have seen what the products can do for them. Because they are satisfied, they have sent referrals to you. When they become a distributor, they will start to earn money from their own referrals. These future distributors have already shown commitment to the products, and will gladly continue to purchase the products, but now at a lower cost.

You show commitment to your organisation by sharing with them all the information that the company sends or makes available to you. You do your own organisational meetings and include the help of your network in conducting various elements of the meetings. You call up your distributors and motivate them when they are down.

Part of this interest will include improving their knowledge and skills, and buying them a copy of this book to assist in the building of their business will help!

We have attempted to include in this chapter much of what 'Leadership' is all about – leading. Taking the initiative, setting good examples and instilling enthusiasm and commitment throughout. In our final chapter, we look at a myriad of different ideas which both you and, as importantly, your network can benefit from. All to ensure, **Now It's YOUR Turn For Success!**

Learning Points From Chapter Eleven:

1. At your training meetings, do you explain the importance of product usage by everyone? Do you explain the need to gather the 'stories' from product usage?

2. I ensure that I contact all new recruits and that within seventy-two hours they have ordered product for themselves.

3. I regularly update my action plans and those of my downline.

4. I understand the need to build my network wide and deep, and I have relayed this need to my downline.

5. I regularly promote and attend company events with my downline.

6. I know which stages my recruits are at, and I deal with them accordingly.

7. I follow the 80/20 Rule as part of managing my time.

Notes:

_____

_____

_____

_____

_____

_____

_____

_____

_____

_____

Chapter Twelve

And Finally…

In our closing chapter we have compiled many of the ideas and beliefs which have contributed towards some of the most successful people in the industry achieving the heights others can only dream of. Whilst these ideas and concepts are aimed at a wide audience, from the new starter to the experienced networker, much of what you are about to read we can produce in a presentation style for maximum effect. These ideas and concepts are quite inspirational in their own way and we hope you too will derive great benefit from them.

Opinion vs fact

Everyone has an opinion… an opinion about everything!

Politics, sport, work, religion, other people – in fact everything.

But in this business everyone will have an opinion about your products and your company and even about *you!* Our concern is that their opinion is based invariably on hearsay and *not* on *fact*. Their opinion about your products may stem from someone else's experience or someone else's friend of a friend of a friend who didn't like the distributor anyway for some reason and has chosen to 'sound off' about them and the product without any real justification. All this means they could ruin an otherwise sound business for you and your co-distributors.

There is a saying that the concerns within the industry are based on 10% fact and 90% opinion. No doubt you have heard of this? These statistics mean that a negative opinion which is held by certain influential people can strongly influence your customers and fellow distributors and if not checked (stopped) could also put self-doubt into your own mind about your decision, the company and its products and that is not a very comforting thought.

They could start sounding off about your products stating they are no good or not reliable or they don't meet your outrageous claims, etc., etc. But at the end of the day it is just their 'opinion' and it is *not* likely to be based on *fact* You will have your own experience – Testimonials – and together with your colleagues' testimonials will be able to clearly provide sufficient evidence to support your facts/story.

If someone said that "If you take too much of product XX you will suffer some painful side effects" how would you respond? You might say something like "I don't know about that; all I know is that I've been using the product for two years and I feel fine. Also, John (?) has been using the product for over nine years and he feels fine and looks good/healthy too!" You don't need to lend any credence to their mis-claims at all. Just support your comments with *facts* and *not* fiction. Be positive as we discussed earlier and the concerns raised will often quickly be dispelled.

You could quote the contents of the particular product in question and show how the claims by the opinion maker can be refuted. However, there is a danger here that you get embroiled in a technical argument which is not necessarily a good thing. Remember, you could win the argument but lose the customer!

You are likely to have behind you an extremely professional and ethical company who strive to achieve the highest standards in both products and service to you and the customers, for the products are very carefully screened and checked to ensure you can have *absolute confidence* when discussing and selling them.

If you have thoroughly completed your research of the company we expect you can also have *absolute confidence* in the company. With all of its experience and the support available both from your immediate upline sponsor to the most senior management of the organisation, you can be sure to get the best possible service. The company may be reputable market leaders in many areas and have sound, proven and affordable products which means you can have *absolute confidence* in them and take your distributorship as far as you want to go…

The facts should speak for themselves and when they do you will realise how fantastic the opportunity is that now awaits you.

Attitude

What is this thing called 'attitude' and why is it so important?

We have mentioned attitude several times throughout this book and invariably it will make the difference between obtaining a sale or not. It is important to understand that your positive attitude when dealing with customers can make a significant impact on the willingness of the customer to buy. Everyone likes to buy from a positive and enthusiastic salesperson – we expect you will have previously experienced the excitement generated by such a salesperson. Compare this to the experience you may have encountered when dealing with a salesperson who has a very poor, indifferent and unenthusiastic attitude.

The good news is there are many useful, catchy, thought-provoking and motivational phrases available, some of which you may have heard in the past. We believe a suitable book with the following topics as headings could be a useful motivational follow up to this one! However, in the meantime we make no apology for mentioning a variety of them here, for they really can provide the necessary extra boost, focus and guidance required to assist you in achieving the success you really deserve! So select the ones most relevant for you, write them down and place in a prominent position;

* "If it's to be, then it's up to me!"
* "Before others can believe in you, firstly you must believe in yourself"
* "Attitude is a state of mind"

And there are more…

* "A journey of 1,000 miles starts with just one step"
* "The pleasure you get from your life is equal to the attitude you put into it"

* "Don't wait for your ship to come in, swim out to it"
* "To be a winner… all you need to give is all you have"

And there's still more…

* "The difference between ordinary and extra-ordinary is the little 'extra'"
* "Obstacles are those frightful things you see when you take your mind off your goals"
* "Attitudes are contagious… is yours worth catching?"

And there may yet be more, but one of our all time favourites is;

"Things work out best for the people who make the best of the way things work out"

From this myriad of catchy statements you will no doubt be able to relate quite closely to several of them. So much so that it might just make that difference to your mental approach to the job. After all, it's the 'mental approach' to the job (and life) where attitude plays such a significant part.

Many things in life try and bring us down: family crisis, financial crisis, environmental crisis – you name it and there will be a crisis for it! But what sets 'positive' people apart is the way they approach such events. Do they run away into the corner and stick their head in the ground? Or do they pretend it hasn't happened and that the problem will go away if they don't face it?

No!! The positive people face the event head on, draw out the positives from it and focus on turning the event into an advantage. They do not dwell on the negative issues – sure, sometimes these have to be faced (even confronted) but they approach these matters with a positive and forceful attitude and this is what will carry them through and upwards onto the next level.

Essentially it's all about retaining a 'positive mental attitude' to both the job and life in general. This will help reduce Stress and free up more of your time as you will not become entangled in the downward spiral associated with negative attitudes and the great amount of time that will be lost continually going over the same ground again and again.

Even a simple daily event like parking the car can cause different people to react very differently: do *you* approach a car park in the undeniable expectation that you *will* find a parking space, and invariably you do? Usually because wherever the space was, you treated it positively and confidently – you actually *knew* you would find a space!

Other people approach a car park with 'fear, doubt and negativity' about finding a parking space and especially doubt in their own ability, and guess what? They don't find one!

We all know someone who is negative – they never look for the good in things, always put things down or write events or products off as a waste of time, or tell you how they could do it better, how things are not what they used to be and anyway, why are you so happy?

These people are not beyond help but they might be if they can't appreciate what is required to change their perception of things and events in their life. The world does *not* owe them a living – they must get up and do the work themselves and/or inspire others to help them do it. Do you think they can inspire others with a negative attitude? *No.*

Begin by looking in the mirror; do you like what you see? One of the quotes shown earlier said "Before others can believe in you, firstly you must believe in yourself"; essentially you must 'like' yourself. We don't mean you must *love* yourself (and there are those who do!) but you must at least *like* yourself, and love will follow. When you like yourself, your belief in your own ability will grow, which in turn will increase your personal confidence, which in turn will increase the extent of your feelings for yourself – it's an ever increasing cycle which feeds on itself continually.

If you have been having a few self-doubts lately or concerns as to whether you like yourself any more take a look at the people who are successful. Do you think they like themselves? As we said earlier, some of them positively love themselves but for all that they *are* successful, and that might be where you want to be as well… so think, act and be *positive.*

We guarantee it will change your life. The changes may happen immediately, but usually it takes a little while for the differences to take effect. Once they start to occur make sure you don't miss them! Most people quickly realise how the changes start to benefit them and their mental approach to the events occurring in their life. Be confident in this approach because it *will* change your life for the better.

If it helps, stick some of these attitude statements on your desk, in your car or wallet/handbag and look at them regularly to remind you of how you want to be and what your aim is in life, and it *will* work.

We are sure you would all rather be around someone who is positive and 'glows' with enthusiasm and ideas and confidence, rather than be stuck next to a person who is always criticising everything and being very negative and destructive. If this is true then why not start today and look for some good in each other? You could turn to the person sat next to you now and say something complimentary about them – but with *sincerity!*

It could be that you like their tie/shirt/dress/hairstyle, whatever; just be complimentary about one element of them and guess what? – both you and they will feel a great deal better.

See how good you feel now, and that's just from making/receiving *one* positive statement. Being positive about people/life/work does help you get through the good, and the occasional bad, day. But then in time and with practice, when we are able to be so positive there will never be any more 'bad' days, will there?

Success in MLM

Essentially, there are four ways to achieve success in MLM;

1. Retailing – sell the products yourself – hard work but possible

2. Recruiting – take on others to do the selling for you – share profits

3. Buy – buy the products for 'personal' use only – expensive

4. Combination of the above

Let's do a simple calculation based on your commitment to do three sales a day where the average sale rebate (profit) is only £2.50 (for some it may be significantly higher):

3 x 20days	=	60 sales a month
60 x £2.50	=	£150.00 a month

If you were to increase the average sale value and thereby the subsequent rebate (profit) the figures could look like this:

3 x 20days	=	60 sales a month
60 x £8.50	=	£510.00 a month!!

Not bad for one month, but how about doing this each and every month and eventually increasing it further still? Perhaps this would not be so easy... by building and developing your own network all this and more is possible.

Some people are happy to sell the products themselves and have no desire to recruit anyone else into the company – that's fine (for some) and there is nothing wrong with the concept except these individuals will never earn anywhere near their potential earnings capacity if they don't recruit others to help with their business.

If you are one of these people, please don't worry – settle back, relax and enjoy the day and try not to let the thought of how much other business you may be losing (or how much money you could be missing) worry you.

You will undoubtedly be missing an opportunity to help provide additional 'security' for you and your family, even a source of income in later years which will provide for you very nicely as you approach retirement. Never mind...

Alternatively, if you are *very* keen to secure financial security and happiness in the future then imagine this scenario;

From the potential 60 customers a month :

* 20 – 30 will become permanent customers
* 10 – 15 could become distributors for you
* At least 2 or 3 of these could become Key distributors

Statistically these numbers are correct. However, you may experience numbers which are at a variance with these. Primarily this is likely to be due to the way you approach each customer and distributor.

Having established your need to build 'Wide and Deep' (Chapter Eleven), the above concept should help clarify why it's so important to build a network, or team of people, beneath you – and how easily this can be achieved.

If you refer back to Chapter Eight, where this process is explained in more detail, you will soon discover how to recruit good quality distributors beneath you and thereby allow you to fully realise your true potential and achieve the success you deserve! It's not necessarily that hard, but then "How hard do you want it to be?"

HOW TO USE THE TOOLS EFFECTIVELY

We've already talked about the different ways to introduce what you do when in a lift or on a train/bus, etc. We want you to consider the other mediums available to you to promote what you do and how you can increase your chances for success!

A) **Three-way calling**

Utilise your upline to assist recruiting distributors who are either undecided or who live a long distance away. A three-way telephone conversation is often the most effective method. Don't worry about asking your upline for assistance because if successful they will also benefit!

B) **Use in-house video**

To assist with a range of different areas from product knowledge to selling skills and recruitment methods.

C) **Presentation Folder**

Effectively used this will assist with your retailing (providing evidence – pictures), in recruiting, and act as your business building tool both now and in the future.

D) **Company Meetings**

You will be aware that the company often holds meetings to promote forthcoming events, new products, new sales ideas or to recognise achievers. Make sure you not only attend but that you ensure your growing 'team' also attend. This way the message and enthusiasm will cascade throughout your growing network.

Ensure you set the example and make sure that it's a good one!

E) **Upline**

You need to have faith in your upline/sponsor. Remember, they have no reason to mislead you because they do not make any money until *you* make money first! They need to attend the training events and should take the business seriously. Their level of success either in the business or with product use will allow you to use them as a 'third party' testimonial. You cannot expect more help from your sponsor than you are prepared to give to your group.

F)   **Literature**

The effective use of the product literature which is available from the company will be of professional quality and shows prospective customers and distributors the range of products and business potential which exists for them.

G)   **Ads/Flyers**

These should *not* be seen as the sole means of obtaining business but viewed as an 'add on' to your main areas of business development. It can produce some useful returns but these are likely to be small.

COMMITMENT

At this stage in your 'career' it could be difficult to appreciate how being 'committed' to *your* business can make a difference, and how significant a difference it can make. Firstly, what is commitment?

How about the Formula One motor racing driver who enters a corner at 180mph – do you think he's committed? We would say so – he has to be committed when he enters the corner to be certain of his path *out* of the corner and ensure he is not left in a heap or lots of little pieces on the track side somewhere. He has completed a great deal of 'training' to arrive at this point and has not just been stuck in the car and told to drive... fast!

The chances are he has not got the time, or the inclination, of even contemplating the 'worst' that could happen, such are his powers of concentration and the application of his skill.

Or, how about the chap who has just jumped out of an aeroplane at ten thousand feet with a parachute on his back – do you think he is committed? We would say so – if he does not pull the rip cord at the right moment he is unlikely to survive the fall, or if he does not land following the correct procedure, he could at least be badly injured. Not a very warming thought!

Once he has left that plane there is *no* going back. So yes, we would say he has to be committed – literally! But again, he will have received a great deal of training first!

So how does this relate to you? We can't imagine too many of you jumping out of a plane at ten thousand feet or going into a corner on your way home at 180mph (or will you?). But if you were to do these things wouldn't you need to be 'committed' too? Of course…

Your role within your company is somewhat different to these examples though, isn't it? Well, in certain respects, *no*, it isn't! To be successful and achieve the things you want from life you *must* be committed – if you think of any successful person throughout history whether in sport, politics or industry, after their initial training the one thing they will *all* have in common is total *commitment* to success.

Your upline should be committed to your success – for if you lose, they lose too. They will have a sincere vested interest in your success, however great or small the 'success' might be, and obviously tied into this success they will have a financial interest also. As in fact you will have when you start to seriously recruit new distributors into the business.

So commit to your business now and as mentioned earlier, invest in the company's literature to assist in the on-going promotion of you, your products and your business. You will be astounded at the results achievable in a relatively short space of time.

Another step to take with your commitment is to become more disciplined with your use of time. How much time do you devote each week to this job? Perhaps when you started it will only have been a couple of hours a week, but as your business develops it is likely to increase to a couple of hours a day, and possibly in the fullness of time it may actually become a 'full-time' job.

How will you handle the increasing demands on your time? We have considered the Time Management in an earlier chapter but for now just remember that managing your time effectively is very much a discipline which will help you in your personal as well as business life. And making the commitment to act on what you will learn from this book is crucial to you achieving the success you desire!

SPECTACULAR vs ROUTINE

Life is full of routine events. Every day you get up, wash, clean your teeth (hopefully), have something to eat, go to work, etc., etc. The next day you will most probably go through the same routine all over again!

Now there is nothing wrong with 'routine' things, in fact they are essential to your everyday life. Most of us could not exist without them. You feel safe, comfortable and at ease when you are doing things you are familiar with; you're on 'auto-pilot' for the most part and quite often will not even realise that you are doing the same things day after day after day. It's just like breathing – you forget that you are doing it but you would be the first to know if you ever stopped!

However, amidst all these routine things we do there is also a need for a bit of *excitement* and a bit of *variety* to liven our lives up. For some this may not necessarily need to be too much, yet for others we live for the rush of adrenaline and those 'No Fear' moments in our life. A visit to a theme park like Disney World will soon satisfy most people for their intake of excitement! (For a while at least.) It's 'Spectacular' fun!!

So what has all this got to do with you as a distributor and recruiter? Listen carefully…

How would you describe the way the last company event was explained to you? Was it just casually mentioned that there was a seminar being held – take it or leave it – or was it 'sold' to you as *the* event of the year, something you could not afford to miss – everyone who is anyone will be there!! (A bit of *excitement* creeping in here and there.)

You need to learn how to master the difference between the 'Spectacular' and the 'Routine'. By creating excitement and enthusiasm for a forthcoming company event you will stimulate a tremendous amount of interest and your downline will flock to attend and when they do they will undoubtedly benefit from the experience and subsequently, guess what, so will you!

You need to explain that the next meeting will be the *best ever* and that your most senior executive is likely to be there or the company's top achiever is likely to be there, and so must they be.

Don't worry about who really will be there. Just make sure as many of your downline as possible are there because you know they will benefit from hearing top achievers talk; whether or not it's the company's *top* achiever doesn't really matter, just get them *excited* and *enthused* and get them to attend.

Think again – did your company do a good job promoting their last event? If you attended, something must have been right. What were you told to expect? Was it a day you were told not to miss? Also, you might have been told that there would be elements of the day that would help you promote your business?

Just as the company or your upline did a great job promoting such an event, you as recruiters need to learn to promote the various company events. You need to understand that these events are not put in place because the managing director needs something to do this weekend. You need to understand that these events are put in place in order for you to take full advantage of what the company represents, both in terms of products available, the compensation plan that is available to you for the successful promotion of these products, and to increase your skills as part of your ongoing development.

You should also remember that the events will take place whether you are there or not. Let us ask you, would you rather sponsor a person, tell them a bit about the company, then let them talk to someone in the hope of sponsoring them, (but remember that your new recruit doesn't yet fully understand the workings of the marketing plan), and they are then in turn going to speak to someone else? Is there a possibility that the fifth person's version of the compensation plan would be totally different from the one that you have come to understand?

If the compensation plan gets distorted, it is possible other bits of information will also be distorted. Let's say you find out about this situation, and you then have to spend your valuable time unravelling this mess. Is this time well spent? We would suggest that this is not the best or most effective way to be building your business.

What are you going to do? Take advantage of the company events and bring your people along. If there is local training and you cannot attend, that does not stop your group from attending. Any information you obtain for meetings, rallies, training days, etc., copy the information and send it to your organisation. What better way to be trained/hear new information/talk to others than to attend company events where the individuals get the information first hand!

These events are there to be used by you, so you need to take full advantage of what is offered to you. From experience you will know how regularly these meetings are held. If you attend the first one on your own, and you know this meeting will be run again next quarter, do you want to attend again, and bring along some of your key distributors? Would you like them to bring people along? We would think you might! You may be working to a tight budget/don't like where you live/don't have a good means of transportation. All of this will be unimportant to the distributor attending a company event. Why?

It will be put together very professionally, and at a cost greater than you could probably have afforded or wanted to pay for, and they can also meet other people just like themselves who have chosen the company as a means to achieve their success, and at the same time exchange some ideas.

You need to sell the *drama* of the company event. Not just, there will be another training session on Saturday again, do you want to attend? But an enthusiasm about who will be there and what they will be doing. You may have no idea who will be doing the training on Saturday, but they have built a business... they have achieved... you just cannot miss hearing what they have to say! You may have heard that person so many times that if you hear them again you may scream, but to that new person, it's the very first time; they are new, encourage their enthusiasm. Do you agree that it is better use of your time to have your growing network attend a company training day at the same time?

A word of caution though... remember that for something to be *spectacular* it needs to be billed as 'something special', something they cannot afford to miss and something that is certainly *not* routine! If they attend what turns out to be a 'routine' meeting on a high this is likely to deflate their enthusiasm, knock their interest levels and possibly create a belief that "...well, if that was supposed to be a 'Spectacular' I won't bother going to another one..." This is naturally a situation you do not want to create so make sure to get the excitement levels and enthusiasm levels right!

When there have been a series of recent events, you need to say "How great the last one was, it was unbelievable! If only they could have been there and heard the speakers/met the people, etc., etc." You should go on to say that "Anyway, the next meeting/seminar will be even better still because... " Ensure that they do not want to miss the next event.

So remember that routine is important and everyone needs it, but managing your time and promoting the 'Spectacular' is what will bring people out and get them excited, enthused and committed to attend. Ultimately, it's what will benefit them and you!

We hope you have enjoyed reading this book and that you have taken away many ideas which will help you build a successful business – even an 'Empire' if that's what you desire!

Before we finish there is one final step you need to take and that is to build and formulate an effective 'action plan' to ensure you take away with you all the things you have learned from this book which are relevant and important for *you!* We want you to turn them into something which will continue to work for you and your network in the years to come...

DON'T JUST SIT THERE...

All the different things that you have learned from this book, no matter how great or how small, will be to no avail if you don't *do something about it!* And the *time* to do something about it is *now!*

What you need is a plan... something that is specifically designed for you, by you and which will ultimately benefit *you.* It should be a plan based on *fact* and not fiction, one that is built around achievable targets/goals and one which will ensure you achieve your desired objectives – more money in your pocket, more money to pay off outstanding loans/debts, more enjoyment from an improved standard of living, more pleasure from increased social activities or more time for the family.

Whatever the benefit, your plan must be designed around a few simple and yet fundamentally **S.M.A.R.T.** principles:

1. It needs to be **SPECIFIC** – what is it you intend to achieve?
2. How will you **MEASURE** its success?
3. It needs to be **ACHIEVABLE**.
4. It needs to be **REALISTIC**.
5. Set a specific **TIME** frame to complete it.

As you can see, you need to be *SMART* when designing your action plan. Make sure it's Specific and detailed. Ensure you know how to Measure the success attained, and agree the target to be achieved. Any target needs to be Achievable and Realistic otherwise people will not commit themselves to it fully, or will just not bother. Finally, you need to ensure a specific Time frame is established, what needs to be achieved and by when!? Remember to commit it to paper/print and *write it down* – this will assist you in 'thinking it through' and it also acts as a way to encourage *commitment* both to the plan and to its success.

How many of you have heard the saying: "You can take a horse to water but you can't make it drink!"? This relates quite closely to all the information you will take away with you from this book. You have learned a great deal, in fact at this stage in your life as a distributor arguably *all* you need to know, but we can't force you to start doing it even though we know from experience that when you do start acting upon and implementing the things we have imparted to you here *you will succeed!!*

It's up to you... our advice would be to stop sitting there and start work on your action plan *right now* – whilst waiting for your bus/coach home, sat on the train going home, even in the car (but please do pay attention to the road first!). You may wish to discuss some of the detail with your sponsor or upline and that's fine. There are plenty of opportunities to work out your plan of action so there can be no excuses – I am too busy/I haven't had the time/I'll do it tomorrow!

One adage we mentioned earlier in this book: "No one plans to fail but quite often they fail to plan!" Make sure you are not one of them. Take away with you today your new-found knowledge and develop the skills; if necessary get others to help you and start using them immediately, then watch it work for you and your network.

Remember;

**"Not everyone will surpass their expectations,
though everyone CAN succeed"**

You really will only get out what you put in. Make sure you give this job your 'best shot'. If you don't give it your best shot you will inevitably 'miss the target'!

By stringently applying these ideas and ensuring you effectively cascade the information down throughout your growing network it will ensure ongoing success is within everyone's grasp. If previously you were 'this close' to being rich, you just got a little bit closer...

Summary

We hope that you have taken copious notes whilst reading this book, and that you will carefully consider and implement all of the different topics we have shared with you. These are all based not only on our own experiences, but on the experiences of many other equally successful individuals who we have been fortunate to work with over the years.

When you have finished reading this book, do not put the notes you have written along with this book in a drawer, and forget about them. We want you to take those notes and regularly read them over and over again, and start to put into action what you have learned. Your results won't happen overnight, and we are not expecting you to take everything and start immediately, or first thing tomorrow. What we are suggesting is that you take the sections that are the most important to you, and work with those first. Then go on to the next one, then the next one, and so on.

In order to put a new plan of action together, and allow for your network to adapt to the changes, you need to expect some of this to take a few months before you see significant changes. Although, depending on the topic, other changes may occur almost immediately. But what will happen is that every month there will be an improvement. Make sure that you share the ideas from this book with everyone in your network, or better yet, make sure that they purchase a copy of this book (or maybe you buy them a copy). The volume will go up, the number of recruits will increase, individuals will have higher personal volumes and success will be that much closer for everyone!

Change will not happen overnight, but the plans for change can be done today, and started from tomorrow.

We would like to take this opportunity to wish each and every one of you the best success in building your organisation, and we hope that you will share this book with each and every member of your organisation to ensure you fully realise the true potential which exists. Whilst the past may have proved difficult for you, and the present only just show signs of improvement, with the help available from this book combined with your dedication, the future is likely to witness the realisation of the potential you hold, for **Now It's YOUR Turn For Success!**

> *"Today you will be twice as successful as yesterday and yet only half as successful as you will be tomorrow…"*

Good luck.

Learning Points From Chapter Twelve:

1.   I understand and explain to my network 'Opinion vs Fact'.

2.   I understand the need to have the 'right' attitude.

3.   I know what tools are available to me and my network, and I ensure that they are used regularly.

4.   I am committed to being successful with my company, and my network is prepared to assist me in the process.

5.   I understand Spectacular vs Routine, and I make sure my network makes use of both.

6.   I *will* make sure the ideas highlighted within this book are used effectively, both in my business and within my network. I understand that until I start to use these ideas they will remain just that – ideas!

Notes:

_____

_____

_____

Appendix

Code Of Business Conduct

As the Direct Selling and Multi-Level Marketing industries continue to expand around the world and move into ever increasing and diversified markets, including; cosmetics, skin care, housewares, household cleaning, food storage, food supplements, personal care, electrical appliances, clothes, toys, arts and crafts, jewellery, books, porcelain, in fact virtually anything which is usable and consumable, more and more countries are adopting a 'Code of Business Conduct' or 'Best Business Practice' for the respective organisations to follow.

This will be designed to ensure that both the organisation and the individual distributor or agent adhere to strict guidelines when conducting business. As the UK market alone generates in excess of £1 billion worth of sales per annum you can begin to appreciate the need to have good and effective 'guidelines' in place.

The Direct Selling Association (DSA) has its own code for members to follow. However, listed below are some of the more common 'guidelines' adopted by most companies around the world. In certain countries, usually the more established within the industry, for instance the USA and the UK, these may be more intensely enforced with specific legislation in place and severe penalties for those who breach them. However, in other countries, generally those who are relatively new to the industry, these guidelines may be less severely applied.

In any event, you should be aware they will exist to some extent, and ensure that you familiarise yourself with the requirements within both the organisation you represent and the country you will be selling products or services in. Usually you will find that if you intend to conduct business on an international basis, across borders or continents, the organisation which you represent will have available, where appropriate, up-to-date information concerning the country which you intend to develop and will make available to you all that is required to begin building your international business network.

Best business practice

Aims:

To help organisations, agents and distributors to operate in an ethical and honest manner and to practise the correct processes relating to their role and function within their chosen industry.

1. Selection and recruitment

a) Any individual representing a company and intending to place a recruiting advertisement should refer to the company guidelines.

b) A company or its representative should not make extravagant and unsubstantiated earnings claims in its advertising.

c) By attending a 'Business Opportunity Meeting' (or similar) it should not purport to the attendee to be an offer of employment.

d) At such meetings, the 'Opportunity' should be fairly described and supportive documentation made available.

e) Actual quoted earnings attained by individuals shall be attributed directly to their activities and not reflect earnings owed to others.

f) A company representative shall not intentionally and maliciously alter, amend or abuse other companies' literature or image.

g) A company representative shall not apply mis-truths, falsehoods or lies about another company's products or services.

h) There should be no payment received from merely recruiting, as per The Pyramid Selling Act.

2. Investment in the business

a) Individuals should not be encouraged to purchase any more stock than they are comfortable with or can afford.

b) The purchased stock should be sold at the agreed price, in accordance with the company guidelines.

c) Unsold stock in 'merchantable' condition, may be returned by the individual for the net purchase price, less a handling charge.

d)   Commissions earned from selling the products or services will be paid in accordance with the company guidelines.

3.   Training and development

a)   Companies should make provisions to provide a reasonable standard of Training and Development for its members.
b)   The company should not make a charge to individuals for attending training sessions.
c)   There may be a charge to purchase product videos and literature.
d)   Where such items are purchased it does not infer a condition for gaining additional help and advice from the supplier.
e)   Refunds may or may not apply – see company guidelines.
f)   If legislation requires it, assistance may be provided with relevant licensing, knowledge and competence requirements.
g)   Additional ' Developmental' courses may be available but often at the cost of the attendee.
h)   The individual should take reasonable care to ensure they maintain an 'acceptable' level of knowledge and understanding.
i)   This level of knowledge and understanding will be defined by the company or its representatives – see the company guidelines.

Summary

As stated above, these are simply 'guidelines' and it must be recognised they will vary from company to company and from country to country, in their intensity and diversity. Different legislation and differing ethics are likely to see some, or many, variations. As highlighted on innumerable occasions, you are strongly advised to check with your company ' guidelines' as to how much of what is listed above applies to you and your organisation. Just be aware of how you can effectively maximise your opportunities for success in the future, for:

'Now It's YOUR Turn For Success!'

Glossary of Terms

Much of the content of this book is self-explanatory. However, to aid your enjoyment and understanding we have provided the following Glossary of Terms:

Agent – usually a self-employed person; generally a term used in Direct Sales and also MLM for the people who promote and sell the company's products or services.

Binary Plan – a relatively new commission plan that does not have any 'Breakaways' (see below) and is generally based on a simple 'Mirror Image' structure of recruiting people in equal numbers. See Chapter Two for a diagram.

Bookings – in Party Plan one of the aims of each party is to elicit guests to agree to have a similar party in their home. For this the hostess will usually receive some small gift.

Breakaway – the word given to a situation when a person you have sponsored reaches the same level as you within the company. No profit is paid to you, but the company will then pay you a Loyalty Bonus, dependent upon your sales and the sales of the Breakaway in any given month.

Direct Sales – a means of bringing the goods direct to the consumer; generally by Direct Approach and selling products or services on a commission only basis.

Distributor – a self-employed person; generally a term used in MLM. Someone who will 'distribute' products.

Downline – a word used in MLM to denote all of the people who are below you in the genealogy of an MLM organisation. You may receive a commission/bonus from the company on the orders placed by some of these people if you have achieved the company targets to receive such payments.

Hostess – the person who has a Home Party for the demonstration of goods. A gift and/or commission is given for her efforts.

Loyalty Bonus – a payment made by the company to you based on the orders placed by the 'Breakaways' in your downline. Payment is made when you have achieved company targets, and the payment is generally paid monthly. Can also be called Royalty Bonus or Override.

Marketing Plan – one of several names (remuneration plan, commission plan) given to the structure of payment as set out by the company for the sale of goods and bonuses on sales achieved in a given period of time.

Matrix Plan – a plan based on a set system of people placed in a 'structure'. Common plans are five people wide by five people deep, resulting in twenty-five people in total to be recruited to receive maximum payment. See Chapter Two for more information.

Multi-Level Marketing – a means of selling products to consumers and recruiting others to do the same. Commissions/bonuses are paid for your efforts.

Network – the name given to the organisation (downline) that you have recruited.

Opportunity Meeting – a meeting open to the public designed to introduce prospective recruits to the opportunities within the company for unlimited earnings.

Order Direct – a method whereby your distributors are able to purchase their products direct from the company or designated stockist. Any wholesale profit or bonuses payable to you are paid by the company at the end of the period, generally a month.

Organisation – a word used in MLM that is synonymous with 'network' and denotes the entire group of people that you have sponsored, either directly or indirectly.

Party Plan – a method of direct selling to a group. Sales are generally in someone's home, with invited guests. Some MLM companies adopt this method of selling.

Pyramid Selling Act – An Act enforced by the government in several countries to prevent illegal trading in an MLM or Direct Sales company.

Recruit – the name given to someone who is newly introduced to the company.

Requalifying – the name given to a situation when you must achieve a predetermined amount of sales within a given period by the company in order to continue to enjoy commission earned from a Breakaway position.

Retail Profit – the difference between your purchase price of the product and what you sell it to the customer for.

Sliding Scale Plan– a commission structure that sees you climb each month through various stages of commission. If the 'top' position is not reached in a month, you then 'slide' back to the starting point for the following month. When the 'top' position is reached, the commission amount remains the same according to the company guidelines.

Sponsor – the title given to someone who personally recruits you into an MLM opportunity.

Step Plan – a commission plan that denotes changes in commission percentages at different stages of someone's progress to top commission level. This plan includes 'Breakaways'.

Upline – a word used in MLM to denote the people who are above you in the genealogy of an MLM organisation. Several of these people will receive a commission/bonus from the company on the sales that you generate if they meet company targets to receive such payments.

Wholesale Profit – the difference between the price you paid the company for the product and what you sell the product to your downline for.

Wholesale Volume Profit – the name given to the 'value' of product ordered by your downline in any given period.

Torgate Training & Consultancy Limited

Co-directors: Richard Houghton and Janet Kelly

A UK based training and consultancy organisation with international experience in America, Canada, Europe and South-East Asia.

We specifically focus on the needs of our clients with an in-depth knowledge of the Direct Sales, Multi-Level Marketing, Financial Services, Estate Agency and Retail industries. We are naturally pleased to discuss training specific to other industries. Our training courses are based around interaction, participation and the development of skills, whilst recognising cultural differences.

Our company and personal aim is to achieve a highly successful long-term business relationship with our clients, providing personal attention to each of their demands; designing interactive training where the learning process continues back in the workplace and is successfully implemented. The results obtained meet the agreed objectives.

Torgate Training & Consultancy Ltd. offer a wide range of diverse skills and have the ability to tailor programmes to suit the individual needs of the client.

Our satisfied clients arise from the various international companies who have attended our programmes, or from where we have completed specific training and/or consultancy, including:

- ❖ Institute of Multi-Level Marketing (IMLM), England
- ❖ BPP, England
- ❖ Residential Estate Agents Training & Education Association (REATEA), England
- ❖ Halifax Property Services, England
- ❖ Harley Davidson of Malaysia Sdn Bhd, Malaysia
- ❖ Panasonic (M) Sdn Bhd, Malaysia
- ❖ Shell Petroleum Co Ltd., Sabah
- ❖ Malaysia Airlines (MAS), Sabah

- ❖ RAYMA Management Consultants Sdn Bhd, Malaysia
- ❖ Lumier Systems, Singapore
- ❖ Dion Cosmetics, Belgium

Please contact us for details on how we may be able to help your organisation to increase sales, productivity and profits!

Torgate Training & Consultancy Ltd.
Torgate House,
29 The Grove,
Haywards Heath,
West Sussex,
England,
RH16 3SJ.

Tel and Fax: +44 (0) 1444 413416

Visit our web site at: http://www.torgate.co.uk
E-Mail: info@torgate.co.uk

Crown House Publishing Limited

Crown Buildings,
Bancyfelin,
Carmarthen, Wales, UK, SA33 5ND.
Telephone: +44 (0) 1267 211880
Facsimile: +44 (0) 1267 211882
e-mail: crownhouse@anglo-american.co.uk
Website: www.anglo-american.co.uk

We trust you enjoyed this title from our range of bestselling books for professional and general readership. All our authors are professionals of many years' experience, and all are highly respected in their own field. We choose our books with care for their content and character, and for the value of their contribution of both new and updated material to their particular field. Here is a list of all our other publications.

Change Management Excellence: Putting NLP To Work In The 21st Century
by Martin Roberts PhD   Hardback   £25.00

Figuring Out People: Design Engineering With Meta-Programs
by Bob G. Bodenhamer & L. Michael Hall   Paperback   £12.99

Gold Counselling™: A Practical Psychology With NLP
by Georges Philips & Lyn Buncher   Paperback   £14.99

Grieve No More, Beloved: The Book Of Delight
by Ormond McGill   Hardback   £9.99

Hypnotherapy Training In The UK: An Investigation Into The Development Of Clinical Hypnosis Training Post-1971
by Shaun Brookhouse   Spiralbound   £9.99

Influencing With Integrity: Management Skills For Communication & Negotiation
by Genie Z Laborde   Paperback   £12.50

A Multiple Intelligences Road To An ELT Classroom
by Michael Berman   Paperback   £19.99

Multiple Intelligences Poster Set
by Jenny Maddern   Nine posters   £19.99

The New Encyclopedia Of Stage Hypnotism
by Ormond McGill   Hardback   £29.99

Peace Of Mind Is A Piece Of Cake
by Joseph Sinclair & Michael Mallows   Paperback   £8.99

The POWER Process: An NLP Approach To Writing
by Sid Jacobson & Dixie Elise Hickman   Paperback   £12.99

Precision Therapy: A Professional Manual Of Fast And Effective Hypnoanalysis Techniques
by Duncan McColl PhD   Paperback   £15.00

Scripts & Strategies In Hypnotherapy
by Roger P. Allen   Hardback   £19.99

The Secrets Of Magic: Communicational Excellence For The 21st Century
by L. Michael Hall   Paperback   £14.99

Seeing The Unseen: A Past Life Revealed Through Hypnotic Regression
by Ormond McGill   Paperback   £12.99

Slimming With Pete: *Taking The Weight Off Body AND Mind*
by Pete Cohen & Judith Verity   Paperback   £9.99

Smoke-Free And No Buts!
by Geoff Ibbotson & Ann Williamson   Paperback   £7.99

Solution States: *A Course In Solving Problems In Business With The Power Of NLP*
by Sid Jacobson   Paperback   £12.99

The Sourcebook Of Magic: *A Comprehensive Guide To NLP Techniques*
by L. Michael Hall   Paperback   £14.99

The Spirit Of NLP: *The Process, Meaning And Criteria For Mastering NLP*
by L. Michael Hall   Paperback   £12.99

Sporting Excellence: *Optimising Sports Performance Using NLP*
by Ted Garratt   Paperback   £9.99

Time-Lining: *Patterns For Adventuring In "Time"*
by Bob G. Bodenhamer & L. Michael Hall Paperback   £14.99

Vibrations For Health And Happiness: *Everyone's Easy Guide To Stress-free Living*
by Tom Bolton   Paperback   £9.99

Order form
*******Special offer: 4 for the price of 3!!!*******
Buy 3 books & we'll give you a 4th title - FREE!
(free title will be book of lowest value)

Qty	Title
—	Change Management Excellence
—	Figuring Out People
—	Gold Counselling™
—	Grieve No More, Beloved
—	Hypnotherapy Training In The UK
—	Influencing With Integrity
—	A Multiple Intelligences Road To An ELT Classroom
—	Multiple Intelligences Poster Set
—	New Encyclopedia Of Stage Hypnotism
—	Now It's YOUR Turn For Success!
—	Peace Of Mind Is A Piece Of Cake
—	The POWER Process

Qty	Title
—	Precision Therapy
—	Scripts & Strategies In Hypnotherapy
—	The Secrets Of Magic
—	Seeing The Unseen
—	Slimming With Pete
—	Smoke-Free And No Buts!
—	Solution States
—	The Sourcebook Of Magic
—	The Spirit Of NLP
—	Sporting Excellence
—	Time-Lining
—	Vibrations For Health And Happiness

Postage and packing

UK: £2.50 per book
£4.50 for two or more books
Europe: £3.50 per book
Rest of the world £4.50 per book

My details:

Name: Mr/Mrs/Ms/Other (please specify) ....

Address: ....

....

....

Postcode: ....Daytime tel: ....

I wish to pay by:

❏ Amex   ❏ Visa   ❏ Mastercard   ❏ Switch – Issue no./Start date: ....

Card number:...Expiry date:...

Name on card:...Signature:...

❏ cheque/postal order payable to **AA Books**

Please send me the following catalogues:

❏ Accelerated Learning (Teaching Resources)	❏ Psychotherapy/Counselling
❏ Accelerated Learning (Personal Growth)	❏ Employment Development
❏ Neuro-Linguistic Programming	❏ Business
❏ NLP Video Library – hire (UK only)	❏ Freud
❏ NLP Video Library – sales	❏ Jung
❏ Ericksonian Hypnotherapy	❏ Transactional Analysis
❏ Classical Hypnosis	❏ Parenting
❏ Gestalt Therapy	❏ Special Needs

Please fax/send to:
**The Anglo American Book Company,
FREEPOST SS1340
Crown Buildings, Bancyfelin,
Carmarthen, West Wales,
United Kingdom, SA33 4ZZ,
Tel: +44 (0) 1267 211880/211886 Fax: +44 (0) 1267 211882**
or e-mail your order to:
crownhouse@anglo-american.co.uk